In-laws and Outlaws

IN-LAWS & OUTLAWS

C. NORTHCOTE PARKINSON

Illustrated by
Osbert Lancaster

John Murray
London

for Ann

Contents

Preface

In making success available for the first time to all, I have some claim to the gratitude of mankind. Whether I receive the thanks I have earned is another matter. It is by way of example, however, that I can do something to ensure it. For if the reader must owe much to the author, he in turn must owe as much again to all who have helped to make this book an accomplished fact. I must thank first the editors of the magazines in which some of the chapters have already, in substance, appeared; *Esquire, Fortune, Lilliput, New York Times Magazine*. Next I must thank my publishers, to whose keen interest I owe far more than I normally choose to admit. My debt to Osbert Lancaster for his vigorous and subtle illustrations must be obvious and is therefore the more frankly acknowledged. I also record my thanks to Mrs Valerie Fitchet who deciphered and typed my manuscript, reducing it to a comparative coherence. I add finally my thanks to Ann, without whom the effort would have been pointless and to whom, for reasons innumerable, this book is dedicated.

C. NORTHCOTE PARKINSON

Easter, 1962

FIRST ENTRY

Books on how to succeed, of which this is the latest and best, are seldom in disagreement about what success can be taken to mean. The expression 'to make good', as colloquially used, may not appeal (and in fact doesn't appeal) to the philosopher or moralist, but it has at least the merit of being understood. We know, roughly, what is meant. We picture the successful man as one with high office, secure future, untarnished repute and a good press; all gained or improved by his own effort. Our mental image shows successively the house by the lake, the mature garden, the daughter's jodhpurs and the Georgian silver. With change of focus we picture the panelled office, the shining desk, the expensive tailoring and the silent car. A last angle shot reveals the exclusive club, the central figure of the central group, the modest disclaimer of sincere applause. For what? Victory, promotion, honours or another son? All four perhaps. That is what success commonly means and that is the sense in which the term will here be used.

It is not to be denied that other forms of success exist, from canonization downwards. Some have given their names to exotic blooms or else dashed off immortal verse. Others have lived to an improbable age or played in concerts from the age of eight. Success can take this form or that. Granted that this is so, the reader must nevertheless expect no more than he will find. If the success in which he is interested is of the sort here first described—

the sleek convertible, the private beach—this book tells all. Should he picture success in terms of reward in an after-life or indeed of posthumous fame in this, he should seek elsewhere. No tips on martyrdom are offered between these covers. Where the word 'success' is used, success in the material sense is intended. But while the success under discussion is material, it is not crude. For our present purpose, the man who makes good has not merely made money. Wealth by itself, without prestige and popularity and marred, perhaps, by parsimonious piety, is merely a form of paralysis. The art of success may involve money but must also involve sliding easily into the governing section of society, conveying the vague impression of having been there all along. In the days when motion pictures used to offer entertainment it was the custom of the impoverished to walk into a cinema backwards through the exit saying to each other, 'That was a rotten film.' In much the same way the technique of success implies an unobtrusive entry into the ranks of the privileged. One must go in with all the boredom of one who is coming out. It is not enough to enter: one must also *belong*.

The advice which follows on how to succeed assumes, then, a special form of success. It also assumes that the reader is an average person but with something less than average ability. We too often see books on 'How to Succeed' in which the student is urged to be more energetic, more intelligent, more helpful, more painstaking, more pleasant and more loyal than anyone else. But if he has all those merits, he has no need for the book. It is not for that sort of person that the book should be written. He will succeed anyway. The person in need of advice is *below* average—stupid, idle, careless, un-co-operative, ill-tempered and disloyal. It is for him that books should be written. After all, this is a democratic country. Why shouldn't he succeed like anyone else? He can, and we shall presently explain how. We shall assume for this purpose that success is to be in a field of activity to which most people are assigned and for which all the others are clearly destined; the field of public and business administration. People imagine for themselves a career in agriculture, research, stock-breeding, literature or field-anthropology. Each sees himself as test-pilot, secret agent, ace reporter or cowboy. All will end, if successful, at a desk; and it seems to make little difference, in practice, whether the desk is at a university, on a rocket range, on a farm or in Whitehall. Come what may, that desk awaits each one of us. We might just as well realize this from the start, beginning as we mean to continue. And once seated at a desk, our problem is how to move from desk to desk until we reach the topmost desk of all.

The reader must be warned, however, against expecting more than the author has to offer. This book includes no advice on how to succeed in politics. On this subject a useful book might be written, but this is not it. A career in politics may have much to commend it but its rewards are reserved, in the main, for those who have been successful already. On the one side of the House, a wealthy family background is not so much required as assumed. On the other, political eminence is hardly to be counted as success at all. Towards grasping the reality of politics a first and useful step is to study *Who's Who*, an invaluable work of reference which includes a short biography of all who could be called eminent in public life.

A study and analysis of these biographies will reveal the

foundation upon which each great career is built. To perform this task thoroughly would mean the writing of a book on that alone. But even a cursory study of a hundred names may suffice to explain the elements of success. Such a study the author of this book has made, the statistical material being provided by the Conservative government of 1955–56. If Ministers and Under-Secretaries are taken, including all who held office even for a part of the period; if to these are added the Treasury commissioners and law officers; and to these again are added the Speaker, the Chairmen of committees, Black Rod and the Serjeant-at-Arms, we arrive without much distortion at the useful total of one hundred. Of this hundred 81 were educated at a public school, 70 at Oxford or Cambridge and 13 at Sandhurst, Woolwich or Dartmouth. Of the public-school men no less than 27 were Etonians, Harrow and Winchester providing only five each, Rugby only three and Marlborough and Uppingham only two. Schools with a single representative included Westminster, Charterhouse, Cheltenham, Radley, Malvern and Stowe. Of the university men, 45 came from Oxford and only 25 from Cambridge. Of the Oxford men, 13 were from Christ Church, and of the Cambridge men, 12 were from Trinity. Of the 13 from Christ Church, no less than 10 had also been at Eton. From statistics of this kind a certain pattern begins to emerge. One may not have been present when the government was formed but one has, from internal evidence, a clear notion of how it must have been done.

It would not be difficult to reconstruct the sort of marking system which must be used in political circles—and this has already been done. Marks are awarded for Eton, Christ Church, the Guards and for a suitable father-in-law,

with a special increment for being related to the Duke of Devonshire. But the Parkinson Scale has also made it possible to draw up the perfect entry in *Who's Who*; perfect, that is, for one just entered on a distinguished political career. It would read something like this:

UPTON-CUMMING, Neville Edmund Windrush
M.B.E. Parliamentary Private Secretary to H.M.'s Secretary of State for Foreign Affairs, M.P. (C) for Alltory (West) since 1953, Director of Upton Plastics, Ltd., Slough; *b.* 1926, 2nd *s.* of the late Arthur Upton and Martha, *o.d.* of Hiram B. Cumming of Pittsburgh, U.S.A ; *m.* 1951 the Hon. Sheila Swellyn, *y.d.* of the 1st Lord Innercausus (*q.v.*) and of Lady Elizabeth, *e.d.* of the 14th Earl of Normantowers (*q.v.*) and widow of the Rt. Hon. Sir Cecil Sleightly-Cavendish (*d.* 1917). One *s.* Sandhurst O.C.T.U. 1943, commissioned in Grenadier Guards, served in Italy, mentioned in despatches and awarded M.B.E. *Educ.*: Eton, Christ Church, Oxford, M.A., 1st Class Hon. Mods., Racquets Blue. President of the Oxford Union, 1949. Barrister, Inner Temple, Major in Barsetshire Yeomanry (T.A.). Travelled in Outer Mongolia, with Public School Expedition to New Guinea, and was correspondent in Korea. *Publications: In Darkest Mongolia, My Plan for Employment* and *The Coming Five Years. Recreations:* fishing, squash, collecting snuff-boxes. *Address:* 203 Cadogan Mews, Sloane Square, S.W.3, and Oakrafter Lodge, near Newbury, Berks. *Clubs:* Carlton, Pratts, Guards, Cavalry.

The discerning reader will observe that the politician to whom this entry refers has a 100 per cent rating on the Parkinson Scale—a score far higher than any real statesman can actually claim. He also has a range of useful adjuncts— a reputation as author and traveller, academic, athletic and military achievement, the Presidency of the Oxford Union and at least one whimsical hobby which seems out of character with the rest. Here is an ideal to aim at, preferably from birth; but the astute reader will have noted that Mr Upton-Cumming has one qualification which his *Who's Who* entry implies but never states. He is obviously *rich*. It is not for him, therefore, that this book is written. He can presumably look after himself. The author seeks rather to help those who began with less, those for whom politics are out of the question.

For success in administration all that we need at the outset is the knowledge of how to cheat in Intelligence Tests and how to dodge the Personality Screen. All this is childishly easy, the tests being designed merely to exclude (and very rightly) those to whom even cheating is too much bother. We shall assume that these tests have been passed and that the reader already has a desk of sorts. What do you do next? The chapters which follow provide the answer. The assumption which seems to underlie the advice given is that the reader is in business and that his ultimate ambition is to become Managing Director of a mammoth Group of Associated Companies. In many instances this may be true, but the counsel offered is just as readily applicable to any other form of administration. One office is much like another and the principles as here laid down will apply to all. Given a desk (the basic need) with in-tray, out-tray and pending, telephone, blotter and memo pad, the technique of success will always be the same. Whatever your actual career may be, whether in governmental, municipal, local or business administration, the same procedures will apply. With this book at your bedside, success is practically unavoidable. For the first time in history, success has been made possible for all.

BACKGROUND

With one foot on the lowest rung of the ladder, your first problem will be to reconcile two quite contrasted policies. On the one hand you must hint at a more than respectable background. On the other, you must avoid spending a penny more than is unavoidable. Don't marry to begin with and don't have a flat. Each evening, as your colleagues leave, they will see your office light still on. Each morning when they arrive they will find you already there. 'How he *works*!' they will say to each other. 'He practically *lives* at the office!' They will be right. That is where you will sleep. You will belong to a club for use at the weekends, and on public holidays you will spend the night at a turkish bath. Your meals at the coffee-bar will cost about 2s. 4d. each. Save and invest every other penny you receive. As regards your background, that should be built up on holiday. For the first five years of your career you should spend the annual two-week holiday as follows: the first two near Eton, Winchester or Rugby, the last three near Oxford, Cambridge or University College. Study the current faculty or class lists, debating reports and football results. Collect copies of the student newspapers. Get to know the porters and groundsmen. Read all the available books and memorize all discoverable maps. Take with you, on one or two of the visits, some ambitious friend who has changed his name to Astor or Cholmondeley. Then begin, very lightly, to touch in the background with snapshot and indirect reference. You are in fact a graduate of Whatsitville Comprehensive School and Wheresit University, and proud of it; but these are circumstances which you need not, for the present, seek to emphasize. On no account must you tell a lie. Nothing could be more wicked, or indeed more foolish. You should aim rather to build up atmosphere. When you say 'I did no rowing at Cambridge—I dare say I worked too hard', you will be telling the truth. When you refer to your friend, Archie Cholmondeley, and add 'We were at Eton together', you will be strictly accurate. There is no need, however, to be so specific. When some pastime like archery is mentioned, you can admit ignorance—'It was not known, I think, at Oxford.' Nor need you have met the film star for 'He wasn't at Univ., was he?' In all indirect suggestion the main rule to follow is this: make up your mind which school it is to be. It is fatal to mix them. You may object that the office building contains somewhere an I.B.M. card punched full of holes, accurately recording your Whatsitville and Wheresit career, with its consistent Class III going back to kindergarten. Don't give it a thought. The office has to have these things as a symbol of status, but no one looks at record cards or does anything but file them. Without making any actual claim, without telling a single lie, without being anything but your modest self, you should become, in five years, that Old Harrovian in the Public Relations Department who works harder than anyone else in the firm.

Background can be lightly indicated but money should be at least partly real. The man who saves his salary will have something to invest; hardly worth investing but useful in conversation. While playing the market cautiously and on the best advice, you should refer, very occasionally, to your large-scale operations, hinting alternatively at spectacular profit and disastrous loss. The gains and reverses will be real, representing your actual speculations, but in sums greatly exaggerated. About once a year you should celebrate your gains by having five of your most talkative colleagues to an incredibly lavish dinner. Remember, however, that a loss is just as impressive. For raising of status, it is the *scale* that matters; whether the total is plus or minus is immaterial. Claim no particular prescience but confess, if you will, to having some luck. The immediate object is not, however, to suggest wealth but to claim kinship with the Astors and Rothschilds. They have their market dealings and you have yours. It may thus become known that you are interested in Polychrome Plastics. 'Not a *controlling* interest?' some awestruck acquaintance will ask. 'Hardly that!' you will reply with a laugh, leaving him to reflect that even 43 per cent (say) of the ordinary stocks would represent quite a sum.

After five years of saving and investing you should have a capital sum at your disposal. There are various possibilities but your best plan is probably to spend it on travel. There is something to be said for quitting business for six months and reappearing with the reputation of one who knows the world. For this purpose you can rule out Europe as too well known. Something might be made of having been to Zagreb, Skopje or Santorin but their prestige value is scarcely worth the effort. Chatter about Cagliari is waste of time. The modern traveller can impress only by casual reference to Faizabad, Kaohsiung or Bandjaimasin. 'That reminds me,' you want to be able to say, 'of something that happened to me once at Ayuthia. ...'

It may occur to you at this point that the Organization Man, as now conceived, needs no knowledge of the world and would be hampered, perhaps, by any knowledge of any kind. This may be the approximate truth but times are changing and you must anticipate what the change is to be. The present fashion for conformity will pass and a temporary demand for individuality will follow. To be outstanding as an executive may be difficult but to have visited Indonesian Borneo is fairly easy. Do something like that and so establish for good your identity as an individual; as the man who has visited Tasmania; as the man who knows the world. Having decided upon this policy you have three alternatives between which to choose. You can visit some territory thought to be unexplored. You can learn some language known to scarcely anyone else. You can, finally, visit some scene of minor conflict and return as a military expert—or with the name of one whose past has included some reckless adventure. The main result of your travels will be a book and it would be well for you to decide in advance what the book is to be about. To travel first and then consider your impressions afterwards is unscientific and leads to the accumulation of time-wasting and irrelevant experience. Study the bookstores and note what is being published. There are fashions, you will observe, in adventure. But there are also good reasons for concluding that the market is, in some directions, overstocked. No one will now approach his publisher with a story of a child brought up among a tribe of apes. We realize that this has been done. Nothing is now to be gained by crossing the Pacific on a balsa raft. Little fame will be derived from a knowledge of the Linyutang dialect. Least of all will service in the Foreign Legion (should it

still exist) justify another book about adventure in Peacy-
wrenia.

With certain avenues definitely closed, you would do
well to test your own prose style before booking your
passage.

> The canoe upsetting meant that all our supplies had been lost,
> with no stores nearer than Madlyrash, our last link with
> civilization. The journey back would take at least sixteen
> days by the river and longer by the other route. The rains,
> remember, would come in three weeks' time. . . . I decided
> to push on.

The technique lies in introducing the row of dots at the
right point. If at all uncertain about this, decide against
the exploration business and emphasize rather your acquaintance with obscure language and customs.

> One of the strangest characters in the vicinity was Sheering
> Venshyan the pedlar from Mehkbeheliv. I saw at once from
> the style of his turban that he came from the other side of the
> hills and addressed him in what I hoped was the right dialect.
> 'Wudyanho?' I began but he merely shook his head.
> 'Comongsaarva?' I tried again and with a similar result.
> But then he solved the problem for me by muttering 'Hoos-
> yersen?' I knew then that he came, at least originally, from the
> north.

Provided you can write this sort of thing, your reputation as a linguist will be established. If you are haunted,
however, as some writers are, by the fear that you will
meet someone who really speaks the dialect you have pre-
tended to master, your better plan will be to concentrate
on the third or military approach. This can be attempted
at two levels, the elementary and the advanced. The
elementary reads rather like this:

All was silent save for the sound of machine-gun fire from the other side of the Sierra. Miguel and I approached the ruined hacienda on tiptoe, looking carefully to right and left. Suddenly Miguel stopped and examined the ground. I kept guard while he did so. Slowly, rising to his feet he whispered, 'Señor, eleven men passed this way within the last half-hour. I think the hacienda will be occupied.' As he said this I heard a faint click as his safety-catch was released. Our eyes met for a moment—perhaps, as we knew, for the last time. With eleven of them against two of us, we should need to shoot straight. 'Vamos!' I whispered and our advance began. . . .

This school of authorship dates from the Spanish Civil War and has been the basis for many a reputation, being readily transferable to South or Central America. Military writing at the advanced level was the invention of the late Mr Hilaire Belloc, who did his service as a peacetime conscript in the French artillery. This made him an expert on strategy, which he still remained even after two world wars had added something to our experience of warfare and little to our veneration for France. It is unlikely that any modern youngster will rival Belloc as a master of English prose but he can be readily imitated as a strategist.

The problem was essentially one of supply. With his railhead at Pnom Penn and the road under shellfire beyond Kompong Thom, General Aix-les-Bains had to move his infantry in at least brigade strength up to the line of the Lam Nam. Unless this were done in six days the post at Cheon Ksan would fall. Now, the distance from Pnom Penn to the Lam Nam is 218 kilometres by the main road. With his advanced troops already at Ph Rovieng it was arithmetically just possible—but only just—for the relief column to arrive in time. The movement began on March 14th and was unopposed until the evening of the 17th, when, at Tamesch . . . etc.

Supposing you have decided to become an explorer, the first thing is to decide on a dust-jacket for the book you mean to write. Exploration dust-jackets are of two kinds: those with bare bosoms and those without. They are designed for different markets, the second type of jacket sometimes taking the form of a map or the silhouette of a mountain range. On an average the first type is better business, provided the girls are reasonably attractive. Selections of such a dust-cover will then narrow down your field of choice among places waiting to be publicized.

These preliminaries settled, the next thing is to define the territory you mean to explore. Once again, it is a mistake to be influenced too much by the character of the country. The better policy is to write your story in outline and then find a tract of scenery which will do as background. Basically your need is for a photogenic tributary with rapids, waterfalls and at least one crocodile. Distant mountains are an advantage and a native village for the foreground. Make an early decision as to whether there should or should not be tigers. As you are not a big-game hunter, you can well do without them. If, however, you think one essential, a good plan is to purchase some still photographs at the Zoo and superimpose them on the negative of a photograph taken locally. Some explorers take a stuffed tiger's paw with them for making tracks in the mud. This is a perfectly sound scheme, for only a trained zoologist will notice that your tracks are all made with the near hind paw: and no zoologist is likely to read your sort of book.

In writing a travel book the thing to avoid is monotony. The only remedy for this is to give your story a climax. In a tale of mountaineering the crisis comes with the conquest of Mount Wothavyu, the cairn built, the flag set up on the summit, the Sherpas buried and the peak evacuated. This happens two-thirds of the way through the book, leaving the last chapters for a somewhat partisan assessment of what the achievement means. At least one chapter should explain why the previous expedition failed through having the wrong climbers, the wrong equipment, the wrong maps and the wrong food—apart altogether from their error in approaching from the wrong direction at the wrong time of the year. But mountains should play only a minor part in the sort of travel book we are discussing. Climbing feats should not be emphasized unless you are an actual climber, which we can assume you are not. It is best to throw in an oblique reference, a faked camera study and a modest disclaimer, passing on quickly to something else. So the climax of your book will not be on a virgin summit or even down an unexpected crevasse. What is the crisis to be?

Of the various climaxes, 'the Fire in the Long-House' is probably the best. It has served many a script writer at a loss how to finish the story and will serve many script writers in years to come. It lacks any touch of originality but it is dramatic, final and neat. It lends itself to vivid description. It disposes of unwanted characters, including the Chief's Daughter (if there has to be one). It can wipe out the whole community if you like, making your anthropological notes impossible to refute. It allows you to rescue someone—the faithful tracker, perhaps, who had never left your side in times of danger—and it rounds off the narrative in such a way as to explain why your exploring days are over.

As I looked back from the ridge towards where the last wisps of smoke were still visible among the tree-tops, I knew that

I should never return. Why should I? It would not be the same. The happy community I had known would no longer exist. As for Hocusp Ozchus the Medicine Man, I should never know now the truth of the legend. Could he really raise people from the dead? Who can say? He certainly could not raise himself. But that he had exceptional gifts I am fully convinced. Whatever his secrets may have been, they died with him. While I am no believer in the occult I must admit that things I have seen admit of no ordinary explanation. There let the matter rest. Turning northwards again, I began the long descent . . . etc., etc.

If the dramatic climax is useful in a book of exploration, it is vital to a book designed to establish the author's reputation as a linguist. The wise author will therefore build this type of book round a central and predictable event. Ideal for this purpose is the coronation of some hitherto unpublicized king. It is best to attend ceremonies of this kind in a journalistic capacity. There is no need to represent *The Times* or the *Daily Telegraph*. You can go as correspondent for the *Mudborough Chronicle* or the *Poultry Fancier's Gazette*. Journals of this character will usually accept the services of anyone willing to go to Ethiopia or Nepal at his own expense. All you need from the bewildered editor is a letter stating that you are *Girls' Own* special correspondent assigned to cover the coronation at Lhasa or Bangkok. That letter is all you need to secure full journalistic privileges—which usually mean sharing a bedroom with at least three other reporters, two from Patagonia and one from Taiwan.

It is the international character of the affair which will afford you the chance to show your linguistic skill. This is best done in a series of modest disclaimers. 'The fact is that

I know very little Serbo-Croat . . .' 'I can understand Arabic but speak only enough for purposes of travel. The Sheikh made it clear, however, that he belonged to one of the stricter sects . . . etc.' 'Any smattering I may have of Urdu was severely tested that day.' The technique is to follow up a frank confession of ignorance by a scene from which your conversational fluency can be readily inferred. Your subsequent candour will then be disbelieved so that further inaccuracy may scarcely be needed. When you come to write your book, however, it is unnecessary to state that you were the special representative of the *Table Tennis Review* appointed on the grounds that table tennis is believed by the editor, on your evidence, to be the Dalai Lama's favourite recreation. You need refer only to 'the famous journal of which I was at that time the correspondent', throwing in one or two references to the 13–1500-word cables you sent off in the small hours as the minimum coverage your news editor would expect. Remember to record your difficulty in rendering the exact meaning of the phrases used. 'This prayer', you will remark, 'means literally "Hail precious stone in the brightly petalled flower"—but the expression (with its finer shades of meaning) is not really translatable.' That will be enough in itself to establish your reputation as an orientalist. Leave it at that and pass on quickly to comment on the cut-glass chandeliers which the Nepalese import from the West and upon which they base their notions of prestige. Always bear your scholarship lightly, as a foible of which you are half-ashamed.

Come now to the third approach, the theatre of war. There is usually some minor conflict in progress at any given time and indeed there are often several, giving you

two or three campaigns from which to choose. In making
your decision you must again be guided by the character
of the book you mean to write. If you are to attempt something on the advanced or Bellocian level, you must find
some campaign with a tangible enemy; one in a position to
fire back. There might seem to be an undesirable element
of danger in this but you must remember that the grand
strategist has no occasion to come within range or even
earshot of the enemy guns. All he needs is a map, an
almanac, a railway time-table, a pair of dividers and a
bottle of cognac. It must, however, be admitted that wars
fought on this scale—large enough to involve strategy but
not so large as to cause real inconvenience—are infrequent.
You may be forced to take your warfare at the lower level.
That is, frankly, less attractive. Even if the other side is in
no position to shoot at you, there will be no avoiding a
measure of discomfort. You must be far enough forward to
collect your descriptive material, whether it is to be desert
or jungle. Given the background, however, the rest is
simple. You have only to listen to all the current stories and
re-tell them in an improved form with yourself as the chief
character. Everything you hear of as happening will have
happened to you. It is the method used by Mendez Pinto
and many another story-teller. There is every sort of classical
precedent for the technique you will use and the result
will be a very fair description of the war; omitting only the
monotony of it, for that is unmarketable. Here, as in other
possible travel books, the best plan is to rough out the
story in advance. The climax will be the ambush in which
the enemy chief dies, riddled with bullets but defiant to
the end. You will be there as a war correspondent—representing, possibly, the *Plymouth Brother* or *Sunday-School*

World—and the reader will be led to suspect that you were leading the patrol in all but name. 'No, Brian,' you will be thought to have said, 'you should head more to the south-east, and meet the track *here*, just below the spot height 237. I *think* you should have a target at about 1500 hours —at 250 yards range. But don't open fire until the *third* man comes into view.' All this should be obvious from the modest way in which you insist on the subaltern being given all the credit.

Half the value of your reputation will lie in your refusal to discuss these past adventures. You must become adept at reticence. 'Do I speak Swahili?' You will murmur, 'Good heavens, no! I have forgotten anything I ever knew. The language I should *like* to know well is Spanish— perhaps I should say Castilian. I expect you know that language, sir?' Or someone else introduces you as 'the explorer'. 'Don't listen to him!' you implore. 'You might think I had been to the Antarctic! Have you read Dog-sleigh's book on the South Pole? There is real exploration for you!' Or, finally, some hostess begs you to tell her friends about your adventures. 'But, really, I have never seen a shot fired. All that stuff I wrote is just too incredibly bogus.' For once in a way you will be telling the truth. Rest assured, however, that no one will believe a word of it.

IN-LAWS AND OUTLAWS

      To have the right background, at least by repute, and to have in addition a name for travel, knowledge and adventure (whether earned or skilfully assumed) is to gain, at the outset, a considerable advantage. Your more humdrum competitors must seem colourless by comparison and barely distinguishable from each other. Still more vital, however, is the next step in your career. Your main difficulty, as you will by now have discovered, is not in forming the right judgement but in reaching a first position in which judgement is required. There are several ways in which this can be done, one being to model yourself on men who have succeeded, another being to take a correspondence course in leadership. But the best method of all is actually the simplest. It consists in marrying the right girl.

How is this done? You must study, first of all, the glossy magazines, in which photographs of desirable girls alternate with photographs of desirable country properties. The day-dreaming and penniless bachelor can pick his country estate—these being all for sale—and then decide whether the girl on the frontispiece would go well with the architecture and scenery as advertised. She sometimes turns out to be already engaged (rather oddly) or even married to someone else. In other glossy magazines girls as exquisite appear in scenes of an elaborate informality. 'The Hunt Ball of the Harkaway, held at Canterley Court. Miss Harriet Forrard chatting with the Hon. Archibald Frankleigh-Sopping.' The day-dreaming bachelor

B

33

decides that she had better beware—Archibald is obviously not good enough. In other photographs Miss Patience Softleigh appears simply 'with a friend'. An occasional girl is shown leading in the winner at Newmarket or holding the cup she has won in the point-to-point. About all these girls there lingers a slight, and perhaps sometimes misleading, air of being available. A bachelor might be forgiven for thinking they were all in the market.

It should be made clear at the outset that these glossy photographs do *not* afford a good approach to the subject you have now to study. To what extent and in what sense these girls are in the market is not to your purpose. The clue to what you want is to be found in the same magazine but on a different page. The principle upon which you planned your travels was to start with the dust-cover of the book which would result. The principle upon which you plan your engagement should be exactly the same. You study the photographs of the Society Weddings and adapt the biggest of them to your own purpose. You may safely assume that prominence will be given to the bride-groom who is judged to be a Rising Man. As that is what you intend to be, you will plan your affairs accordingly. Should the photograph reproduced on page 17 reproduce a scene outside the Guards Chapel, with a double line of brilliantly uniformed officers making an arch of swords for the Happy Pair—Captain the Lord Utterleigh Broke with his bride the former Miss Penny Lespender—you will realize that your wedding will have to be different. If you were in that sort of position you wouldn't be reading a book like this—nor probably reading a book at all. No, the picture to interest you should have a caption worded somewhat as follows:

Neville Upton-Cumming with his bride, the Hon. Sheila Swellyn, after their marriage on May 14th at St Margaret's, Westminster. The bride who wore . . . was given away by her father, Lord Innercausus. The bridesmaids were the bride's cousins, Miss Prudence de Benture and Miss Marion Fermgilt-Edgerton. The Viscount Hardcurrency acted as best man and the guests included the Duke and Duchess of Cannonstreet. . . .

Study this picture carefully and you will conclude, correctly, that the bride's father is the central figure, Mr Upton-Cumming being essentially his son-in-law. After giving the matter some further thought you will realize that Society is largely composed of sons-in-law; a fact which has only recently been established and one of which only a few are as yet aware. The fact for a rising man to grasp is that your father is given you and there is little you can do about it; but your father-in-law you can choose. Upon the choice of a father-in-law much of your future career may, moreover, depend. Assuming that you have successively made yourself a public school man, a traveller, a graduate and businessman, you have now a crucial decision to make. You must choose your father-in-law, first looking round carefully to see what fathers-in-law there may be available. To list the sources of information which should be consulted, to analyse their authenticity, to arrive at a reasonably accurate process of assessment and to define the principles upon which a selection should be made—all this would be a Ph.D thesis in itself. All that can now be attempted is to dispel some illusions and propound a few basic axioms.

First, as regards illusions, the suggestion has been made that men of ability actually tend to produce more daughters than sons. For this theory (except possibly as applied to university professors) the evidence would seem to be insufficient. Such evidence, moreover, as we possess tends rather towards a different conclusion. If it can be assumed, for example, that those recently raised to the British Peerage as Barons are men of distinction, influence and wealth (an assumption which might admittedly be challenged) the statistics of their offspring might be thought significant. Of 100 Barons created since 1937 and still alive, some 23 are childless; and not unreasonably so in the case of those who have never married. The remainder can boast some 215 children between them, of which total 112 are or were male, 103 are female. Allowing for a percentage of war casualties, we might conclude that Barons as a race are self-perpetuating but not much more than that. The biology of Dukes, Marquises, Earls and Viscounts is by no means the same and has been dealt with at length in a volume entitled *Fauna of the British Isles*, the work of a well-known zoologist. It is for that reason that the sample hundred Barons excludes those subsequently raised to higher rank in the Peerage. Numbers in the Baronial family appear to range from 1 to 8, the commonest total being 2 or 3. What is depressing about the statistics, from the bachelor's point of view, is that only 13 Barons have daughters only and of these only 5 have restricted their female offspring to one. With only these 5 definite sole heiresses and 8 more with younger sisters to consider, the field is not and has never been extensive. And from this discouragingly low total we must make deductions in respect of those over fifty years of age, those who turn out to be bankrupt and those—probably the remainder—who are married. It would be rash to generalize on the basis of these figures, but further research would almost certainly justify our tentative conclusion that the chances of inheriting baronial estates by marriage are relatively low. The sons are far too numerous and the only daughters are far too few. These are the sad facts and there is no escaping them.

It has been emphasized, in the Introduction to this work, that some examples of success in life, although inspiring, are somewhat unhelpful. When a list of Ministers is seen to include such names as these, the Marquis of Salisbury, the Earl of Selkirk, the Earl St Aldwyn, the Lord De L'Isle and Dudley, the Earl of Home, the Marquis of Reading, the Earl of Munster and the Earl de la Warr, the reader may have his moment of despair. He may think that the plan for his success should have been made at some earlier date, preferably perhaps some four centuries before. The advice 'Be born the son of the 5th Marquis of Salisbury' is undeniably sound: but is it useful? Some reader might be in that favoured position but it is not for him that this book has been written. Nor are books on how to succeed intended for people born as sons of the 13th Duke of Hamilton and Brandon. These can presumably look after themselves; nor do they form, for book-buying purposes, a sufficiently large public. The advice here offered is for men of an entirely different type, for men of ambition upon whose choice of a father-in-law much else will depend. It has been shown that their chance of inheriting vast estates by marrying an heiress is fairly remote. What they can do—what the reader of this page can do (if unmarried, male and reasonably young)—is to marry into a family with influence.

The reader may wonder whether this is really feasible. It certainly *is* feasible and it is constantly being done. Turn the pages of the illustrated magazines until you find the group picture of the House Party at Macsporran Castle. Ignore all the chief figures in the scene. Our concern is not with the Earl and Countess of Macsporran nor with the Mackintosh of Mackintosh nor with Lord Pipeslament, nor even with the Honourable Jean Tartan. Look closely, rather, at the two young men who complete the group; Mr Nigel Smyth and Mr Christopher Browne. It is not obvious, to begin with, why they are there at all. Why ask Smyth and Browne rather than Robinson, Baker and Jones? What have they which others lack? The matter is not without its element of mystery, but the fact of their ubiquity is undeniable. By some obscure process, the presence of Smyth and Browne has become inevitable. There they are, each with his tweeds and his 12-bore, and neither looking particularly abashed in the presence of the nobility. They look more as if the grouse-moor belonged to them, which it certainly does not. These Smyths and Brownes are the future sons-in-law, the Men of Promise. The question is how you are to gain a place among them? One useful step is to learn how to ride and shoot. We may be sure that the Mr Smyth who emptied both barrels of his gun into the kilt of Lord Pipeslament would never be invited to the castle again. It must, however, be admitted that this necessary training is not in itself the entire secret of success. If every marksman were invited to Macsporran in August, the moor would be unduly crowded; a fact which the Earl and Countess will have realized. Nonchalant handling of firearms may be essential but it is certainly not enough.

In approaching this difficult problem the first axiom to observe is that you need not try to impress the entire nobility. There are young men who appear, no doubt, on every possible occasion and in every conceivable guise but we can safely assume that you are not to be among them. Your better plan will be to choose your father-in-law and then begin your campaign from there. Your problem is not to impress the whole peerage but gain the good opinion of one important man. Who is it to be? The choice would be simpler if the possible names had been collected in a single work of reference, but nothing of the sort has ever been done. You will have realized without prompting that your list of possible fathers-in-law must be confined to men *who have daughters*. Many a young man has sought to ingratiate himself with a wealthy brewer or newspaper proprietor only to find him to be childless or the father, merely, of innumerable sons. All this results from sheer carelessness and deserves no sympathy. The man whose respect you must gain must be influential, wealthy and the father of at least one daughter. One with several daughters is, of course, preferable, your chances being thereby multiplied.

Let us suppose that you have drawn up a short list of six. They are, shall we say, a Scottish Peer who has recently become Postmaster-General, a Baronet of ancient family with a seat in Parliament and an extremely wealthy wife, a Football Pool Magnate, the Sultan of Gushing-Arabia, a Greek shipowner and the proprietor of the *Sunday's Wonder*. Let us suppose that the Postmaster-General is, for some reason or another, the man you think most suitable. Let us suppose, further, that he is known to have three unmarried daughters; Angela, Barbara and Caroline, born in alphabetical order and aged respectively twenty-six, twenty-three and nineteen. Their father, the 4th Earl

41

of Bonniebanks, owns the Clanwhiskey estates in Ellesdeeside and has extensive interests in the Argentine, Canada, Panama and Nicaragua. The family seems suitable in every way. Which daughter is it to be? The deciding factor is age. A wife should be half her husband's age plus seven. If you are aged twenty-four, you should try to secure Caroline; if thirty-one, Barbara; and if thirty-six, Angela. Should you have planned your career with care, Caroline might be first choice, with Barbara as reserve. This policy decided upon, it only remains to make yourself known to the Earl and Countess; but that, for the unenterprising, is the main obstacle. For the reader of this book, however, it need not be insurmountable. The paragraphs which follow should be studied, therefore, with more than usually close attention. One of the better-known experts on modern warfare writes frequently about the Strategy of Indirect Approach. Whether that is a good idea in warfare may be matter for dispute, but the principle is one certainly applicable to the problem now under review. To charge up to the Earl and say 'I want to marry one of your daughters' would be a tactical error. The occasion is one for strategem, subtlety and finesse. And the essence of the technique is to obtain the fullest information beforehand.

Begin your research by listing and making full notes on the Earl's and Countess's nearest relatives; their names and whereabouts; their special interests; and whether they are on speaking terms with the family concerned. Let us suppose your card-index entries read like those opposite.

There would actually be more than eight entries but these few are enough to illustrate the principles by which you should be guided. First, decide which is the more

	Name	Family Relationship	Real Relationship	Special Interests
1	Viscount Clanwhiskey	Earl's first brother	Mutual loathing	Breeding angora rabbits
2	Lord Ellesdeeside	Earl's second brother	Neutral	Master of the Deeside Otter Hounds
3	The Hon. Philip de Canter	Earl's third brother	Intimate with Earl	Collects old duelling pistols
4	Lady Crystal de Canter	Earl's only sister, unmarried	Neutral	Vice-President of the Society for the Prevention of Practically Everything
5	Mrs Heather Tartan	Elder sister of Countess, married to No. 6	Intimate with Countess	Enthusiast for Stuart succession
6	General Douglas Bloodworthy Tartan	Brother-in-law of Countess, married to No. 5	Friendly with Earl	Deerstalking, salmon fishing, describing how he won the First World War
7	Miss Ailsa McGaelic	Unmarried sister of Countess	Hostile to everyone. Detested by Earl	Practises Yogi. Spends much of her time in Tibet
8	Miss Bloodworthy Tartan	Sister of No. 6	Friendly with Countess	Headmistress of St Agatha's College for Young Ladies

formidable—the Earl or the Countess. Let us suppose
that it is the Earl you chiefly have to conciliate. The
possibilities between which you have to choose appear to
be these:

1. You can write an article to prove that the breeding
   of angora rabbits is a vice beside which the crimes of
   Nero fade into insignificance.
2. You can find an unusual pair of duelling pistols and
   ask No. 3 to identify them.
3. You can join the Jacobite Society and ingratiate
   yourself with No. 5.
4. You can write to No. 6 and ask his opinion as to how
   the First World War was won.
5. You can allege that No. 7 has never been to Tibet, or
6. You can lecture to the College for Young Ladies of
   which No. 8 is the Headmistress.

There is nothing to prevent you trying all these ap-
proaches simultaneously. The artistic touch would be to
lecture to the Young Ladies' College on Old Firearms,
ensuring that Nos. 3, 5, 6 and 7 are present. Use the rare
duelling pistols to illustrate the lecture, with an angora
rabbit as the target. Kill the rabbit with the first shot and
wound Aunt Ailsa accidentally with the second. End the
lecture by pointing out that the Stuart kings never bred
angora rabbits and that the First World War was nearly
lost by the kind of people who do, but won at the eleventh
hour by people with experience of deer-stalking. If you are
not invited to Clanwhiskey Castle after that, it will be
clear to you that the family is not worth bothering about.
The chances are, however, that you will find yourself an
honoured guest within a matter of weeks, and Caroline

will probably be told to marry you whether she wants to or not. Should there be any sales-resistance on her part, you can probably secure Angela by pretending to be interested in Barbara. The engagement announced, you will shortly enter the select ranks of the world's sons-in-law. Two moments of triumph will mark the process even before the wedding takes place. First of these will be marked by the appearance of the group photograph:

> On the moors at Ellesdeeside. The Earl and Countess of Bonnie-banks, Lady Crystal de Canter, Mrs Heather Tartan, the Hon. Philip de Canter and General D. B. Tartan, D.S.O. (Seated) Lady Angela and Lady Barbara de Canter, with Mr Christopher Browne and Mr Aubrey Reeder.

Second will be the appearance of a portrait on the first page of a later number:

> Lady Angela de Canter, whose engagement has recently been announced to Mr Aubrey Reeder, the prospective candidate for Alltory (West).

The photograph will be extremely flattering, having been taken some six years before. Elsewhere in the same issue will be a charming picture of Swindlesham Manor, Sussex, the home of Mr Aubrey Reeder. Does such a place exist? Almost certainly, one would imagine, but there is no need for you to own it. A Manor is easily borrowed and a picture of one can be borrowed more easily still.

As from the date of your marriage at a fashionable church you will be definitely *in*. Why? Because your wife's relatives cannot afford to have failures in the family. Their affection for you may be strictly limited. Their affection for her may tend to diminish. But their own credit is involved, to some extent, in your success. For just as you will refer to them, casually, as relatives, so they cannot avoid referring (less frequently) to you. 'The Supernational Banking Corporation?' you will say, 'Of course I know it. My wife's uncle is the Chairman.' 'Dorset? No, I have never been there. My uncle by marriage keeps a pack of hounds there, however, and I'm looking forward to our first visit.' 'Salmon fishing? I never had the time until last year, when General Tartan invited me to his place in Scotland.' To be able to make these references may gain you nothing more than prestige. But what when business acquaintances ask Lord Bonniebanks about Angela? 'Shall we be seeing your married daughter at Ascot?' and 'How's your son-in-law doing?' and 'I hear, Lord Bonniebanks, that you have a grandson. Congratulations!' For the sake of his own status, your father-in-law cannot afford to have you anything less than a Director. With whatever misgivings, he will have to see that you are promoted.

You are now one of the world's In-Laws. But what would your fate have been had it happened otherwise? You would have been a No-Law or an Outlaw, and these are terms which we must now define. A No-Law is an eligible bachelor, one who must make his way unaided but about whom there lingers the romance of one still available. There are minor advantages in this role, provided you are not too low in the firm's hierarchy. The typists will work for you more willingly and the mothers of the less attractive girls will ask you to parties. Rumours may circulate about your broken heart, about the heiress to whom you were engaged but who died of diphtheria, about the starlet who finally married someone else, about the French Countess whose family forbade the match on religious grounds, about the Austrian Princess who entered a convent so as to avoid being married to your rival. Such rumours will go around, provided you originate them, and will do you no harm. Neither, however, can they do you much good. As compared with an In-Law the No-Law is in a weak position, any hint of mystery about his past being as likely to repel as attract. Minor advantages apart, his main asset lies in the fact that he may still become an In-Law. As compared with the Outlaw, the No-Law is at least a potential Man of Promise. His cards are still to play.

Hard is the lot, by contrast, of the Outlaw. His mistake has been to marry the wrong girl. This comes about, normally, through marrying at too early an age. He never forgot that blonde at the Comprehensive School. He remained loyal to the brunette he loved at College. He fell for the redhead who typed his first letters as a young executive. Whichever it is, he has tied himself by marriage to the environment from which he is trying to escape. The Mudborough School blonde is attractive only by the standards of Mudborough, which are of course appallingly low. The College brunette may have been the best of the bunch at Liverpool—but what a dreary bunch that must have been! As for the office redhead, she is merely the smartest girl of the five who are still unmarried. It is the itch to marry the girl next door which is the mark of those predestined for merely average success. For while such a wife may be anxious, in general, for you to succeed, she will not want your success to go beyond a certain point. She will retain her Mudborough outlook. In a larger circle of more prosperous friends she would find herself below the average in looks, family, brains and knowledge.

Her unspoken preference is for a society in which she can be well above the average. Down to that level she will try to keep you and the odds are that she will succeed. It is thus usually fatal to marry the girl next door. To this rule there is one significant exception. A woman sufficiently beautiful can make her way at any level of society. Married to a girl of stunning appearance a man may have his moments of anxiety but he will not, in general, find that she hinders his career.

Nubility or fitness for marriage can be measured by a formula, here to be revealed for the first time. It depends upon careful investigation and survey. Where this is impossible, however, or where a snap decision is needed, the generally accepted tests can be applied in a shortened form. Look at her eyes to see what a girl was born with. Look at her hands to see what she has learnt. Look at her mouth to see what she has become. There can be no pretence at accuracy in this hurried valuation but it follows the same pattern as the more careful assessment. It is obviously preferable to apply the test at leisure, aiming at a precision which we know to be finally unattainable but using nevertheless such science as we can. From the table which follows it will be evident that there are eight general aspects of quality. They can either be positive, with values graded from A to D, or negative from E to H. Using the methods of simple arithmetic, a man of any ambition should normally reject any idea of marrying a girl whose negative qualities outweigh the positive so that $E + F + G + H > A + B + C + D$.

Girls with a zero score are not and should not be in great demand. Girls with a positive rating will have a score from 1 to 100, obtained by simple addition, the result being the

N.R. or Nubility Rating. These totals give us, in turn, the Nubility Classification (N.C.) as follows:

Totals	Class
100–85	I
84–70	II
69–55	III
54–40	IV
39–25	V
24–10	VI

Girls with a score below 10 are unclassified.

The Male Nubility Rating is obtained by using the same table, substituting 'good appearance' for 'beauty' in Category A and 'Salary, status and prospects' for 'income and expectations' in Category D. A man who fails to qualify had best forget the whole idea and turn at once to the next chapter. One who qualifies, however, can fairly decide how high he should aim. A Class III man could thus reasonably dream of securing a Class II girl, while a man in Class I might normally hope to marry a girl in Class I.

But the man for whom this book is written, the man who seeks to rise in the world, is rarely in Class I, having lost marks heavily in family background, knowledge, disposition, popularity and income. He is probably in Class III at best. But his policy, as we have seen, is to marry a girl with a good family background, ignoring the fact that her N.C. may be as low as IV. He thus becomes an In-Law. Had he, however, married the girl next door, he would probably have found himself with a wife in Class V or VI. This would automatically make him an Outlaw, having married

Category	Plus Factors	Marks	Totals
A	Health and Beauty Vitality and Energy Intelligence	20 10 10	40
B	Good Family Background Athletic Skill and Aptitude Knowledge	20 5 5	30
C	Loyalty Good Disposition and Manners Social Ease and Popularity	10 5 5	20
D	Income and Expectations	10	10
			100

Category	Minus Factors	Marks	Totals
E	Poor Appearance and Health Idleness and Inertia Stupidity	20 10 10	40
F	Unpleasant Relatives and Friends Carelessness and Clumsiness Ignorance	15 10 5	30
G	Infidelity Quarrelsomeness and Bad Manners Snobbishness and Unpopularity	10 5 5	20
H	Extravagance and Indebtedness	10	10
			100

two or three Classes below expectation without any
compensating factor from his wife's background. It is not
to be denied that Outlaws occasionally succeed in life but
for this they need quite exceptional gifts. An In-Law can
succeed, by contrast, with gifts below the average and

indeed with no obvious merit of any kind. It is for this reason that such emphasis is given here on the question of marriage. For should you make an early and unsuitable marriage or should your plans for becoming an In-Law go astray, you will have to rely only on Yourself in what you will find to be a highly competitive world.

NONORIGINATION

As a young business man you should learn early in life that your advice is of no value to your elders and betters. It is normally futile to approach them with a plan for reorganizing the business, for such a plan implies that it needs reorganizing—the most insulting suggestion one business man can make to another. And even were the suggestion acceptable from anyone, it would not be acceptable from *you*. Who are *you*, a mere deputy assistant, to tell the directors how their business should be run? Submit your memorandum, expecting promotion to result and you will find yourself before the Managing Director but not merely to receive his congratulations.

CHIEF: Reading this memorandum, Mr Reeder, I find myself wondering who is the chief executive here, me or you.

REEDER: You are, sir.

CHIEF: Me? But I evidently know nothing about the business. After thirty years as a manufacturer, I still need guidance (it would seem) from the most junior people in the office. Does this strike you, Mr Reeder, as unusual?

REEDER: Yes, sir; I mean, no, sir.

CHIEF: You think, perhaps, that my methods are out of date?

REEDER: No, sir. Certainly not, sir.

CHIEF: You realize that I have had years of experience? And you realize that you have had none? But you still think that you know best?

REEDER: Yes—no—I mean yes, sir.

CHIEF: You realize that staff have been sacked for making suggestions only half as insolent as these? Do you expect me to be more lenient with you?

REEDER: No, sir—yes—I mean, no, sir.

CHIEF: (*Gently and quietly*) Merely for your own good, Mr Reeder, I advise you to keep your ideas to yourself until you have more experience. Try to believe that those senior to you know what they are doing. Try to recall that this business was conducted, somehow, before you were born. Try to imagine that it could go on without your help. Try to learn, reflect and consider. In the meanwhile (*suddenly screams*) GET OUT!!

This type of interview does nothing to hasten your promotion or ensure your peace of mind. It is best for that reason to approach the whole matter from a different angle. We shall suppose, for this purpose, that your scheme is perfectly sound and will save the firm half a million each year. In putting it forward, you can have three possible objects. First, you can add to the Company's prosperity. Second, you can gain the reputation of being clever. Third, you can so alter the hierarchy's structure that your own position becomes more important—as, for example, in creating a new post which only you can fill. The first two of these objects you can dismiss at once. The Company's prosperity (unless it is actually tottering) is none of your business. A reputation for cleverness is the last thing you want, nor could it lead to anything but trouble. Only the third object could justify your taking action. And there are, even then, two major pitfalls of which you must be aware from the start. In the first place, your motive is likely to be obvious. In the second place, the new vacancy may go to someone else. You will end, if unlucky, with the reputation of an intriguer and of one whose intrigues fall completely flat. This is not the sort of reputation you wish to establish.

How often did it happen during World War II that a Lieutenant-Colonel (General Staff) would produce a reorganization scheme by which a headquarters establishment came to be considerably expanded. Accepting the scheme for which he had pleaded so eloquently, the General would gaze at the new organization chart with the appreciation of a connoisseur.

'Yes, yes, yes,' he would mutter as he adjusted his spectacles. 'A very effective solution to our difficulties. I notice, by the way, that this establishment includes a vacancy for a Brigadier.'

'The upgrading became essential,' the Lieutenant-Colonel would admit with a modest cough. 'It followed from the readjustment of duties at the Grade II level.'

'Just so, just so,' the General would murmur. 'Upgrading becomes inevitable. I shall have to make a recommendation.'

Blushing slightly and glancing downwards the Lieutenant-Colonel would begin to word the letter he would be writing home. 'It came,' he might say, 'as a complete surprise. . . .'

'Yes,' the General would repeat sadistically, 'I shall

have to make a recommendation . . . and I know the very man. Brigadier Coldsteel of the First Parachute Division, one of my oldest friends. He comes out of hospital next week. The very man! (*Telephones*) Get me the base hospital. . . . All right, I'll hold on. . . .' Turning once more to the Lieutenant-Colonel, he would add, brightly, 'And now I have *another* problem. What am I to do with *you*?'

This is not the sort of situation in which you should place yourself. It is essential, therefore, that any scheme you originate should be put forward by someone else who honestly believes that the idea was his in the first place. Neither praise nor blame need come your way, nor can it be thought that you stooped to intrigue. Of all the administrative techniques there is none, probably, of more importance than the art of having your views put forward by someone else. Towards this desirable result the first step is to choose your stalking-horse. It must be somebody to whom the Managing Director will listen, somebody fairly senior, somebody who is open to suggestion and somebody without too many ideas of his own. There is such a man in every organization and we shall call him Harry Bumbling. He is a keen member of the Golf Club and it is there that you will push your acquaintance. Your attitude from the start must be one of humble admiration. 'I wish I had your knowlege of the business,' you will sigh. 'It must take years of experience to develop your sureness of judgement!' 'How strange,' you will protest, 'that a man of your seniority should retain so youthful and fresh an outlook!' Before long you will be able to insist on his daring and original ideas. 'There is no one but you who could have thought of that, Harry. We all know by now where the Managing Director gets his ideas!'

Having established a relationship as of master and disciple you wait for the next occasion of festivity and waylay Harry Bumbling in the Cloakroom. You need to be rather more sober than he is.

'Gosh, Harry, this scheme of yours for making K Division a separate Company—I think that's a wonderful idea!'

'What scheme?'

'Mike has just told me about it. In strict confidence, mind you. And do you know what I said?'

'How could I? I wasn't there, was I?'

'Well, I said to him, "Mike," I said, "that man's a genius!" Did I mean it? I'll say I meant it.'

'You meant what?'

'I meant it when I called you a genius.'

'Why?'

'Because of your scheme for K Division.'

'What scheme?'

'For making K Division a separate company—Mike told me about it.'

'Who is Mike?'

'Mike Bablock. But I realize it's secret and he shouldn't have told me.'

'Of course it's secret. Why can't he keep his mouth shut?'

'He *does* talk too much. But the scheme is splendid. The most astute idea I ever heard—from the tax angle alone— yes, Harry, a stroke of genius!'

'What is?'

'Your scheme for K Division.'

'Oh, that. But keep it under your hat.'

'Strictly between ourselves. Let's have a drink.'

'Good idea. A brainwave!'

'No, you're the man for brainwaves. The rest of us are not in the running.'

'Who said I was running?'

'I never said you were—Oh, never mind. Let's go and drink to your scheme.'

'What scheme?'

If you handle the matter correctly, old Bumbling will emerge from the party with a vague idea of having discussed something of momentous importance with somebody. Next day he will wonder what he discussed with whom. It will be for you to remind him and preferably over the telephone. This will set the rumours going from the Head-office switchboard.

'That you, Harry? I think I should tell you there has been some leakage about your scheme for K Division— the idea we were discussing last night. Everyone is talking about it. They all think it quite brilliant.'

'Brilliant? Oh, I wouldn't say that. Basically quite a simple idea.'

'A simple idea which occurred to no one else! Actually it was the application of the scheme which impressed me even more. You have the thing worked out to the last detail.'

'Have I? Well, I mean, it doesn't do to be vague.'

'I was so impressed, Harry, that I made some notes as soon as I got home. I hope they are an accurate account of what you had in mind.'

'Perhaps you had better send them over for me to check.'

'I'll do that right away. Another thing though. Two difficulties occur to me. You will know the answers, I'm sure, but I feel bound to point them out. Would you be interested?'

'Yes I should. Let's meet for lunch. At 12.30 in the County Club.'

'Thanks very much. That will be fine. It's very good of you to discuss Company policy with me. Junior as I am, I can contribute nothing. But I am keen to learn.'

'Glad to give you any guidance I can. At 12.30 then. Good-bye.'

The arrival of your notes, incoherent as they may be, will solve Bumbling's main problem for him. He will know what it is he is supposed to have suggested. There will be nothing particularly clever about it but nothing manifestly unreasonable. There will be several inaccuracies in your notes and he will automatically correct them. At least one word will be misspelt, over which he can smile. 'These young fellows don't know everything!' He will see at a glance how things could be put into shape and paragraphed properly. Not a bad scheme, though. With the pencilled correction, he will be accepting responsibility for it. With each improvement the idea will become more definitely his.

Over lunch you will raise your two objections. These must be prepared with considerable care. Although just plausible enough to arouse interest, they must admit of a quick and final answer. One could be a point in law, something about Company registration in Northern Ireland. 'But the new Company', says Bumbling, 'will be registered in Canada!' 'But of course!' you will exclaim.

'How stupid of me to forget that!' Your second objection can be a little more difficult, something about raising the capital for expansion, investors no longer having the security offered by the Group as a whole. This will be another skittle to knock down, probably at the second shot. The object of this manœuvre is to give Bumbling the sensation of victory. He has overridden two objections to his scheme. Who will oppose him next? A further object is to dispel any lurking suspicion that the whole idea is really yours. Why, the stupid young fellow was against it at first—could do nothing but think up difficulties! Very helpful since, mind you, and worked hard over the scheme in its later stages. Under good direction, might be a useful Assistant-Manager. Not too much initiative as yet, but that may be a good fault. There is nothing more intolerable than a young man who thinks he can run the Company. Young Reeder knows his place—that is something in his favour. Originality may come with more experience. He might have a future—who knows?—as Manager. Yes, a useful man.

So the originator of the scheme receives none of the applause? None at all. He must reject from the outset the least suggestion that the idea came from anyone but Bumbling. This is in accordance with a general principle of administration. Always have your ideas put forward by someone else. The man in control of the committee is often the man who says nothing. Pursue the opposite policy, advocating a scheme and expecting to gain credit by its adoption and you may well succeed—just once. By that one success you will have created the opposition to anything else you may propose. With the reputation of being too clever by half, you will be side-tracked into work of lessening importance. Your career, at least in the Company which you first joined, will end before it has begun. Your only policy will be to start afresh, having read this book, and make a different impression on a different group of people. In the new firm to which you have transferred there may well be someone to whom the Managing Director will listen, somebody fairly senior, somebody who is open to suggestion and somebody without too many ideas of his own. He is a keen member, as it happens, of the Golf Club and it is there that you will meet. Your attitude from the start will be one of humble admiration. . . . You may know nothing of the business but you will know something, by now, about human nature.

EXPERTIZE

In the course of your business career you will hear constantly of experts on Organization and Method. You will eventually meet them and wonder, perhaps, whether this is a career which you might yourself adopt. You will have realized, after all, that doing a job is more difficult than telling someone else how the job ought to be done. The temptation is a real one but it should be resisted. Let there be no misconception about this. Nothing in this book should be taken as a reflection on the experts in Organization and Method. But that vocation is not for you. As against that, you will often have to deal with Business Consultants. You would do well, therefore, to study their habits and make yourself fully acquainted with the nature of their business. They have come to form a permanent feature of the business landscape, prominent, vociferous and inescapable.

There are many consultants whose respectability is beyond question and many others against whom nothing has actually been proved. More than that, the business of consultation is on the increase. To the industrial firm the expert in method is the equivalent of the psychiatrist and the tranquillizer, being called into play when the strain is proving too much for its constitution, equilibrium and nerves. Just as the troubles confided to the psychiatrist are lessened by being shared, as also by the realization that they are far from unique, so the feverish pulse of a large organization will slow down when the business consultant appears and before he has uttered a word of advice. 'Yes, yes, yes,' he will murmur soothingly. 'Lights burning late in the office, friction over the parking facilities, ill-tempered behaviour at lunch; all the well-known symptoms—just like a case I attended last week.' But the bedside manner is not the whole of his stock-in-trade, nor is sympathy all he has to offer. Sooner or later he will give positive advice—and that is what leaves us puzzled.

In a business organization headed by a Managing Director of eminence, run by directors of experience and overflowing with executives of proved competence and zeal, it must always seem strange that consultants should have to be called in from outside to advise on how the work should be distributed. If the directors don't know how to organize the concern it seems fair to ask what they do know and for what, indeed, they are being paid. It is also natural to wonder what reason there can be for supposing that outside consultants should know what the Board do not. These questions, which have long baffled the public at large, would seem to deserve an answer.

We can reasonably assume, to begin with, that the consultants know very little. Their right to advise derives essentially from their initial act in putting up their nameplate: 'Sneering, Shockwell and Foggarty, Business Consultants', or 'Sadleigh, Deep, Loring and Muddleworth, Efficiency Engineers'. Everything has to have a beginning and, for the methods expert, this is it. What were Foggarty and Muddleworth doing before they proclaimed their expertize? This is by no means apparent. They may have taken a correspondence course. They may have attended a class at the London School of Economics. They may merely have failed to earn their living in any other way. But whatever their precise experience has been, there they are, experts in expertize, self-proclaimed magicians of the business world. Hardly has their bronze tablet been screwed to the door-post before the first leader of industry is hammering for admission. As the queue forms in the corridor the skilled observer will note that the gathering crowd of business executives includes few, if any, representatives of the government. No General is there, pausing in the midst of a campaign and anxious for advice as to whether he should withdraw or attack. No Admiral has rushed ashore to sob his troubles into a sympathetic ear. And if the Prime Minister is among those jamming the entry, we must conclude that his disguise, at least, is good.

The middle-aged men blocking the pavement are drawn almost solely from the world of industry and commerce. They are qualified, decisive, tough and keen. The Chairman of the firm which makes a celluloid goldfish knows just how his product should be manufactured, advertised and sold. The Managing Director of the firm which produces plastic balloons knows more, it is said, about elasticity and bursting-point than anyone else in that mammoth industry. The Sales Manager of Lollipops Ltd is unequalled in his grasp of stickiness, timber, sugar content and colour preference. There is no one in the crowd who does not know his business. And yet they all seek advice, as it seems, of Sadleigh, Deep, Loring and Muddleworth. Why, for heaven's sake? What does Sadleigh know about celluloid? As little as Deep knows of balloons or Loring of lollipops. What magic formula is it that these experts have to sell?

A careful survey has now established the fact that the clients who approach a business consulting firm do so with one of two motives. On the one hand, they may want scapegoats for the reorganization upon which they have already decided. On the other, they may want to prevent such a reorganization taking place. The contrast between these two procedures can best be illustrated by reference to two recent case-histories. For obvious reasons the identity of both the firms and their Business Consultants will be concealed under names which are purely fictitious. Of the two Companies concerned, the first we shall call the Horseless Carriage Co. Ltd, mass-producers of veteran cars. The second we shall call Historic Homes Ltd, mass-producers of pre-fabricated homes, each with a pre-fabricated story of how Queen Elizabeth I slept there and with whom.

The directors of the Horseless Carriage Company of Coventry decided recently to streamline their organization. They decided, therefore, to sack half their executives and demand some real work from the other half. Their problem was how to do this without being tarred and feathered in the middle of the Company car park. In order to avoid this, they agreed that their proposed reorganization should be the work of outside consultants, so they called in Messrs Sneering, Shockwell and Foggarty and explained briefly what advice they expected to receive. In such a situation as this, the consultant's chief advantage is that he need not linger on the scene. He presents his report with one foot in the jet aircraft's door, reaching 20,000 feet before anyone has finished reading the first paragraph (which consists entirely of thanks to all for their co-operation). These particular consultants work as a team. Once briefed on what the policy is to be, they go swiftly into action. Sneering is condescending in a super-silly way—'Is that your *latest* I.B.M.?' 'You have never heard, I suppose, of marginal costing?' and so forth. Shockwell is direct and brutal. 'You carry absurdly swollen overheads,' he says firmly. 'You should cut down by 52 per cent.' Foggarty follows up with an involved explanation of why the changes are necessary. On this occasion the results of their incursion into the business can be tabulated as follows:

(a) Half the executives were sacked.
(b) A digital computer costing £1,000,000 was acquired as a symbol of progress.
(c) All partitions were demolished, making a general office out of the space previously occupied by individual offices, and
(d) The office colour scheme, which had been primrose and white was changed to lilac and grey.

Very different (at first sight) was the influence of Sadleigh, Deep, Loring and Muddleworth upon the organization of Historic Homes, Ltd. The directors of Historic Homes had been under pressure from a group of shareholders, whose noisy spokesmen, Barker and Maybite, insisted that the firm's organization should be modernized. What exactly they meant by this proposal was never very clear but they did not scruple to suggest that the directors were grossly overpaid considering that their responsibilities concerned only an unmodernized firm. Faced by this dangerous movement, the Chairman called in the experts. Their instructions, on this occasion, were to report that the organization (except in one or two minor respects) was already perfect. In this other group of consultants there is a different allocation of work. Sadleigh shakes his head, Deep looks profound, Loring specializes in a subtle compromise between a roar and a leer, and it is Muddleworth who enters into an obscure and involved explanation of why the changes are essential or (as in this case) needless. As a result of their incursion into the business, the following changes were made:

(a) Messrs Barker and Maybite became Directors.
(b) A digital computer costing £1,000,000 was acquired as a symbol of progress.
(c) The general office was divided up by partitions to form individual offices, and
(d) The office colour scheme, which had been lilac and grey was changed to primrose and white.

There would thus seem to be a complete contrast between the advice given in these two cases. Such a contrast there may be, but the point of significance is that, on both occasions, the efficiency expert did something which the directors could not do for themselves. In the one instance they took the blame for a purge which would have been impossible for those who had to live afterwards in the same neighbourhood. In the other instance their function was to assure the shareholders that the whole organization had now been modernized (whatever that means) and that there could be nothing more to worry about. As regards the partitions and paintwork it would be wrong, incidentally, to suppose that any of the experts had any strong preference either way. Their object was simply to demonstrate that something had been done.

While the two case-histories just outlined are clearly typical, it would be a mistake to assume that the experts never have anything more useful to say. No one with experience in teaching could make that rash assumption, for he must instantly perceive where the consultants have another advantage. Every teacher must at some time have had the experience of being asked, at short notice, to examine in some subject of which he knew practically nothing. To the novice such an abrupt request may bring a moment of dismay. To the older teacher, it is no more than a nuisance, for he knows how the situation should be handled. When the scripts arrive he sorts out the half-dozen which appear to be legibly, neatly and competently done. Reading these, he soon discovers what the right answers are supposed to be, at least for the purposes of that particular examination. Then he marks down the others for giving answers that are different and so presumably incorrect. In the same way the efficiency engineer has opportunities for comparing one organization with another. He guesses which are the best and can then criticize the others for not being the same. In this way his advice, if it is really wanted—and it very occasionally is—can be surprisingly sensible.

Biologists tell us that trees and plants are pollinated by the bees as they pass from one to another—a process now often mechanized but still essentially the same. The efficiency expert is the bee of industry, buzzing from one industrial plant to the next and pollinating as he goes. Many a bee will stoutly maintain, no doubt, that the pollen is his own invention, perfected by a secret process unknown to the other bees. Such a bee is a liar and so, normally, is the consultant who pretends to have ideas of his own. The ideas, like the pollen, come from another plant. And the intensity of this cross-fertilization is in proportion to the number of the bees. Bee-keepers still living can recall a period when they had to pay a rent for bee pasture. With a fuller knowledge, it is now the orchard proprietor who may have to pay the bee-keeper for his co-operation. In these circumstances the bee populations will increase. Business consultants do the same, the fact that they are in demand being proved by the fact that they are in such large supply. And there are all sorts of situations in which, lacking their help, a business man could seek advice only from his competitors. The point may have been reached, however, when the experts have become too numerous. That would be no proof, however, that bees are useless in themselves. Granted that pollination may become excessive, it remains true that pollination must be done.

A problem which remains is to decide how the bee knows a good flower from a bad. Granted that the business method consultant will carry ideas from one organization to another, how are we to know that the ideas chosen are the best? If the examiners can find what the right answers are from a glance at the handwriting, by what similar method can the efficiency expert choose any one organization as a model for the rest? And our anxiety on this score is intensified by our knowledge of what happens in school administrations. It is a known fact that school inspectors, buzzing from one school to another, collect the worst schemes from each and make them compulsory for all. How are we to know that business consultants do not do the same? It would be unethical to reveal all the secrets of the profession, but this is a point on which students seem fairly entitled to reassurance. And the secret, in this instance, is perfectly simple. Among the really expert, all

organizations are instantly judged by the looks of their female office staff. Manager A, who cannot find an attractive girl for his outer office, is most unlikely to have found anything else. His filing system can be condemned without so much as a glance. What should he do about it? Why, he should adopt the system used by Manager B, whose secretary is obviously a darling. We don't know or care what his system may be, but it was the choice of a man whose discrimination has been proved.

Remember, however, that the attractiveness of the secretary must be of the right *kind*. A sultry siren is no better as an efficiency symbol (and is possibly worse) than a frumpish middle-aged spinster. Where waves of a powerful scent surge across the office, lapping against the filing cabinet and spilling into the corridor, the organization is liable to suffer. A deep V neckline can lead to a cleavage among the male staff. Such may be the effect of a swaying exit that hours can be wasted in getting to the bottom of the trouble. The office, we can safely conclude, is not the place for the more powerful manifestations of sex. Neither is it the place for the sort of sexlessness which amounts to hostility. The highest competence is associated with a bright and friendly relationship, the affection felt towards a favourite younger sister, the sister's pride in the achievement of her favourite elder brother, and a popular girl's trusting attitude to the world at large. All this can be sensed in half a minute at the reception desk. Even more quickly sensed are the opposite signs of self-consciousness, frustration or frivolity. In the presence of a frump or a siren, the expert knows at once that the organization is in a bad way and ripe for reform.

What ought to be done—apart from installing a digital

computer and apart from erecting (or demolishing) the partitions? The expert casts his mind back to the last efficient factory he saw; that, as it happens, of the Tinned Cabbage Company, where the blonde receptionist was well above average. Demure and pretty, simply dressed and knowing everything, eager to help and quick to smile, she was obviously a girl in a thousand. Now what was the decor at the Cabbage Factory? Her background, surely, had been a pastel shade of green. How would it be to begin the present reorganization with a change in colour scheme?

PUNCTUOSITY

To understand the principles of Business Efficiency, as laid down by the experts, is a useful qualification for the rising executive. This qualification you now have. Principles, however, are not enough in themselves. You must also pay attention to daily practice; of which the first rule is to be there on time. The rule is of general application but is more especially vital in committee work. Nor can there be any doubt that committees are to play an increasing part in your life. There are industrial organizations, we know, in which all committees have been abolished by top-level decree. But this is a rule more easy to proclaim than enforce. In any normal society the laws of nature will apply. Committees will multiply in number and increase in size. Your own importance may even come to depend upon the number and status of the committees to which you belong. And you will achieve nothing in committee until you have learnt the art of Punctuosity; an art which, at a lower level, is called punctuality. As the following dialogue will serve to illustrate, punctuosity means rather more than being there on time. It means being there on time *and properly briefed*.

CHAIRMAN: Let's see now. Are all members present? There should be nine, I think, apart from Dick. We have eight. Bob, Arthur, John, Leslie—where is *Stephen*? Yes, he's the missing man. Perhaps, Dick, you had best give him a call. In the meanwhile, let's get down to business. May

I take the Minutes of the last meeting as read? Any amendments? Right. Thank you. Now, gentlemen, I shall propose a slight change in the agenda. In view of the urgent need to make a decision on Item 4 I should like to take that first, going on afterwards to Items 1, 2 and 3. Item 4 concerns the alteration proposed for No. 10 Warehouse. We have all read the architect's report, perhaps with some surprise and concern. We also have before us the estimate from the engineers for the air-conditioning plant—an estimate which includes some very surprising figures. I shall say no more at present. The question is, however, do we go ahead or do we reconsider the whole scheme? A decision is urgent as affecting the whole estimate for the division. Far more urgent, in my opinion, than Item 1, which concerns merely the demolition of the disused fuel store so as to make more parking space. We must try and reach a decision today. (*Enter Stephen, breathless, confused and armed with the wrong file.*)

STEPHEN: My apologies, Mr Chairman, I was delayed by some important business.

CHAIRMAN: Very well, Stephen. We have only just begun. You will find a copy of the Agenda in front of you. What was I saying? Ah, yes. The matter is urgent and we must try to reach a decision. We are particularly glad, Stephen, that you could spare the time to come. And we all realize how important your other business must be. For this matter concerns the department of which you are acting head. Perhaps we should ask your views at the outset?

STEPHEN: (*Stammering*) I feel we sh-sh-should go ahead, Mr Chairman. In view, I mean, of the urgency. (*He*

*fumbles with the file, one dealing with workers' accident com-
pensation.)*

CHAIRMAN: (*Surprised*) In spite of the architect's report?

STEPHEN: (*Unhappily*) Yes. I mean, no. There's much
to be said on either side. But the matter, as you said, is
urgent.

CHAIRMAN: We certainly need to make a decision. *That*
is urgent. But the engineer's estimate comes to more than
the original cost of the building. You think we should
ignore those figures?

STEPHEN: (*Lost*) Well, not exactly. Oh, no, certainly
not. By no means.

CHAIRMAN: But you consider, nevertheless, that we
should go ahead?

STEPHEN: Well, we need the parking space … don't we?

CHAIRMAN: The *parking space*??

BOB: (*Gently*) We are discussing Item 4, Stephen. Not
Item 1.

STEPHEN: Oh! I see. Yes, of course. Item 4. I didn't
realize that Item 1 had been dealt with. Well, now. Item
4 …

CHAIRMAN: (*Patiently*) May I assume that you have
studied the document circulated yesterday—the architect's
report and the engineer's estimate?

STEPHEN: (*Lying*) Of course, Mr Chairman. Naturally.
And I am as concerned as you can be over the question of
cost.

CHAIRMAN: Cost is only *one* aspect. The first question is whether the scheme is feasible? Is it? Or isn't it?

STEPHEN: Exactly, Mr Chairman. That *is* the question. I couldn't agree more.

LESLIE: Well, sir, I for one am convinced by the report and feel that the scheme should be abandoned as uneconomic.

ARTHUR: I can't agree with you there, Leslie. The report reads to me like nonsense.

JOHN: That goes for me too. Rubbish!

CHAIRMAN: Remember, gentlemen, that we also have the engineer's estimate.

JOHN: So we have. And I suggest we call for another one from a different firm.

LESLIE: What if we did? And what if the new estimate were 10 per cent lower? The scheme would *still* be uneconomic. Don't you agree, Stephen?

In this imaginary discussion Stephen is completely at sea. He had not forgotten about the meeting, nor about the documents he would need to study. But he had allowed other matters to take his time. The result was that he was late for the meeting—perhaps three minutes late. In itself, the lateness did not matter. What was fatal was his state of disorganization. He would have done better to telephone his apologies and come ten minutes late, armed with the right file and having had five minutes to glance through the documents. The unlucky Stephen will never recover his poise while the meeting lasts (the chairman will see to that) and his prestige will be at a low ebb by the time the meeting ends.

Punctuosity would seem to be the most obvious of virtues, the very foundation of ordinary competence. It is not, however, quite as simple as it seems. For the punctual person has substituted a process of subtraction for the simpler process of addition. The important meeting is at 11.45. Punctual Peter takes that as his fixed point and works backward. He must leave his office at 11.40, check his brief-case and contents at 11.30, give instruction to his deputy at 11.25, having transferred incoming telephone calls at 11.23. That leaves time to see Mark (allow ten minutes)—at, say, 11.10; and Mac (allow fifteen minutes for a Scotsman) at 10.55. There are two important telephone calls to make, six and three minutes, so it is best to start dialling at 10.45. Allow fifteen minutes for reading the report and estimate (Item 4 on the agenda), so bring the file in at 10.30. That brings the normal daily staff meeting forward to 10.15—get Bridget on to that now. Time is 8.55, which leaves one hour and twenty minutes for the day's correspondence. Is there anything that matters? Yes, there is the memorandum from Bagworth—no time to do more than make notes on it. The letter from Doddering —that must wait. Here's *this* thing—tell them 'No' Mary, politely but definitely 'No'. As for *that*—on the whole 'Yes'. Tell them O.K., but not before the 28th. O.K. to this note but 'No' to that one. Put in some explanation— other commitments and so forth. File these three, no answer needed. I'll deal with these two now. Throw the rest away.

That, as we all know, is the way to do it. But the less competent Stephen did it the other way. Starting at 9.0 on the stuff in his In-tray, he worked forward from there, with so long for this and just time for that—which brought him, unbriefed, to the meeting at 11.48. He was adding instead of subtracting, which means being late and disorganized. This is what we all know in theory but find it difficult to apply in practice. There are obstacles and many of these are women. Why? Because the housewife and mother has to work on a different wavelength. For her, things happen differently. Little Jimmy falls out of bed at 5.45 a.m. Little Joan has a sickness, which may be measles, may be tonsillitis—best keep her in bed. Rodney has overslept but must catch the school bus. Gosh, the milkman left us a pint short! There's the telephone—'Myra, dear! But how nice of you to ring up! But it was we who enjoyed having you! The recipe? Oh, it's quite simple, really, but you need an electric mixer. Can't find it now but I'll call you back.' Jimmy has fallen off the stepladder. Joan wants a drink. Is that the baker?—tell him only *one* small brown loaf. Doesn't the vacuum cleaner work? Try giving it a kick. There! The first time that happened, I thought it was the fuse. But one kick, not *too* hard, will usually fix it. Oh, dear—Jimmy has fallen into the dustbin! Yes, he has cut himself this time. The sticking plaster is in the bathroom cupboard—no, it isn't, though—I was using some yesterday and left it in the kitchen. There's the telephone—'But Mr Wilkins, you *promised* to keep the pink toilet rolls in stock! Please do get some ordered. All right, six of the others.' Joan has upset her jigsaw puzzle over the bedroom floor. Rodney! What are you doing here? The school bus broke down? All right, I'll run you over in the car. Keep away from Joan, though, it may be infectious. Which reminds me, I must telephone the doctor. 'Hallo, Margie! Thanks dear, I'd love to come over at eleven. See you later.' There's the telephone again —'Myra, dear! Oh, I *did* give you that recipe? Well, that accounts for my not being able to find it. Good of you to ring up. Good-bye for now.' Rodney! But I *told* you to keep *out* of Joan's room. What did you go in there for? You mean you *want* to catch the measles, so as to dodge your exam? Really, this is utterly disgraceful—I'll have to speak to your father about it. Come to think of it—you *had* the measles last year and can't have it again. Oh, dear— what's that? Jimmy has fallen into the dustbin *next door*!

This is the housewife's day and it cannot be organized. There are too many factors. There is no beginning and no agenda and no one can say when it finishes or what has been achieved. So women work on a different wavelength and it is no good pretending otherwise. Except for those broken in to office routine, or those who have been un-sexed by it, punctuality is not even an ideal. It is not something of which they see the use. The result is that the unpunctual people in the world are numerous, which makes the punctual minority more fussy still. From trying to be five minutes early on principle, they go on to being ten minutes early in practice. This so aggravates the un-punctual that they come ten minutes late from a mere sense of duty. In theory at least they could reach a point where they never met at all. But in matters of unpunctu-ality, as in some other affairs, a known tendency will go into reverse after a certain point has been reached. To be five or even ten minutes early is, or can be, a sign of efficiency. To be half an hour early is to defeat the object of the exercise, not saving time but wasting it. Paradoxic-ally, it can even end in the fussy person being actually late.

Take the instance, for example, of a traveller who is to

arrive at London Airport from New York, taking off forty minutes later for, say, Hamburg. There is barely time to make the connection but it can be done if one plane is on time and the other not too strict, the customs reasonable and the distance short. But life, as we know, is not like that. The plane from the U.S.A. comes in eleven and a half minutes late. The customs regard the traveller's urgency as the oldest trick of the lot. Frantically the traveller races down endless corridors and ends, too late by the clock, at Gate 22. But he is in time. The flight has not yet been called. Will he take a seat, please, in the lounge? Panting and perspiring, the traveller finds a chair. Thank goodness the Hamburg flight has been delayed! He begins to recover his temper and breath. Next announcement comes at 6.25 p.m. (thirty-five minutes later). 'P.C.A. regret to announce that their Flight SK 734 to Hamburg has been delayed for operational reasons. A further announcement will be made at 7.30. Thank you.' This promise is strictly kept and the new revelation is as follows: 'Here is an announcement for passengers to Hamburg holding board-ing cards XYZ. The delayed flight SK 734 has been again postponed for technical reasons. A further announcement will be made at 8.15. Passengers who present their boarding cards at the buffet will be given light refreshments with the compliments of P.C.A.—the tea being dreadful and the coffee, if anything, worse. Thank you.' Announce-ments, at 8.15, at 9.10, at 9.35 and at 9.55 express P.C.A.'s regret for further delays due to psychological, sentimental, physiological and habitual reasons respectively. Then, at 10.20, comes a final announcement. 'Will passengers booked on the delayed flight SK 734 to Hamburg please assemble at the Inquiry Desk, where they will be given further information regarding their flight?' Once assembled they are told that the flight has been further postponed for meteorological reasons. There is fog over Hamburg. So take-off will now be at 7.15 a.m. Passengers will be accommodated in London and can claim their luggage on the floor below. In order to reach the airport at 6.30, arrangements will be made to call the passengers at 4.30. After breakfast at 4.45 buses will leave the hotels at 5.15, weather permitting. Daybreak sees the passengers back once more in the airport lounge.

The first announcement of the new day is as follows: 'P.C.A. regret to announce that their delayed flight SK 734 is now subject to further delay for what we may now call traditional reasons. There will be a further announcement at 8.40. Thank you.' By this time an eternity in limbo and a mutual hatred of P.C.A. have made the passengers friends. Nearest the traveller from the U.S.A. is a fellow victim who admits to being a P.C.A. official. 'Since we have time,' he says, 'let's go and visit the control room.' They do so and the officer in charge explains how the system works. He is faced by a semi-circular wall on which all flights are shown, together with all cancellations and postponements. 'Take your own flight, for example. What is it? SK 734, to Hamburg. It will be over this side. Ah, here it is . . . but, good heavens, you have missed it! It left five minutes ago!' And so it has. It went with all the other passengers at 8.25. Having only fifteen hours to spare the traveller has missed his plane!

The point of this story is that being too early is no safe-guard against being too late. It is the person with hours to spare who misses the boat, and for the good reason that he has time to do something else. Failure to concentrate on the main object can be fatal. It is the ideal plan, therefore, to be a little ahead of time but not so much as to be distracted by the temptation to do this and that—sending a telegram, writing a postcard, changing some money and having a drink. Concentration is the secret of many types of success, punctuality included. It is a good plan to concentrate and to gain a reputation for punctuality. Be there on time with the right file but not conspicuously early— for that looks inefficient in another way. If you arrive early, having allowed for traffic delays which on this morning were mysteriously absent, hide somewhere near by and stroll into the conference with just three minutes to spare. But what if your name for punctuality is spoilt by your subordinates? What if your office lets you down? This is all too possible and the result is a scene of confusion.

'Linda! I want that file for the Staff Committee!'

'Sorry, Mr Scatterleigh, Miss Pelling has not yet arrived. Would the file be in her office or yours?'

'In hers. Do we have the key?'

'Mr Findlater has all the keys. I'll ask him to bring them.'

'Thanks, Valerie—and do hurry!'

(*Five minutes later.*)

'Sorry, Mr Scatterleigh. Mr Findlater is not yet here.'

'Then what am I to do?'

'Well, Miss Lade used to have that office in Mr Oldman's time. She is now in the Accountant's office but might still have a key to the room Miss Pelling uses. I could ring her up.'

'All right—do that. The meeting is in five minutes!'

'Very well, Mr Scatterleigh. (*Into 'phone*) Give me two-five-seven-three, operator, please. Is Miss Lade there?

Very well, I'll hold the line. They are fetching her to the 'phone, Mr Scatterleigh . . . (*long wait*) What's that? She can't be found? Do you mean she hasn't come? Oh, I see —she is somewhere else in the building . . . Is that Edna speaking? I thought I recognized your voice, dear. How are you? That's good. You don't happen to have seen Linda, by any chance? What, you *have*? She just looked in? She did? Well, where was she going, for heaven's sake? She was? Then we don't need Mama after all. What's that? Why, I mean Miss Lade, of course! We always used to call her Mama in this office—short for Marmalade! Never to be found at breakfast, you know. Fancy you not knowing that! What do *you* call her then? Marcia? My, that's funny! I must remember that. No more now, Edna. See you on Thursday. G'bye. Sorry for the delay, Mr Scatterleigh. Linda should be on her way over.'

And what of Mr Scatterleigh by this time? Has he gone to the meeting, telephoned his excuses or died of apoplexy? The one thing certain is that he cannot arrive in time and properly briefed. And the fault is his. He has never discovered how to make other people arrive in time. And yet it is all very simple. The secret is to fix all appointments in terms of the odd minute. Tell someone to report at 10.30 and he will come at 10.36. For him and for most others, 10.30 is a little before the coffee break and means anything up to 10.45. Call the staff meeting at 2.0 and people will be arriving up to 2.10. For some of them, at least, 2.0 means after lunch. More than that, all the hours and half hours are deemed to stretch by ten minutes either way. But fix the interview for 9.29 and the man will be punctual. Call the meeting for 10.13 and that is when people will be there. Tell your secretary to have the papers for signature at 3.03, and that is the time at which she will appear. Why? Because, first of all, the precision used would seem to indicate a fantastically tight schedule with time allotted to the nearest minute. There is also a feeling of curiosity. Why should we have to be there at 10.13 exactly? What will be happening until 10.12? Is the timing really that close? They will be there to find out. And they should then be made to realize that you have a three minute trans-atlantic call booked for 10.09; and another, by the way, for 10.29. This leaves sixteen minutes for the meeting but no time for argument. An important visitor is expected, of course, at 10.32. Everyone, it is clear, must be on their toes.

Will the odd minutes lose their effect as time goes by? Will people cease to be hypnotized by 11.17 and 4.43? Will punctuality wane as the novelty is lost? Probably not. Should this happen, however, the remedy is known. Introduce the half minute into your schedule. Alter the time of the staff conference from 10.13 to 10.12½, explaining that the importance of the business would seem to justify spending another 30 seconds on it. Are people going to regard this as absurd? For the time being, they may. And the niceties of timing will eventually have to disappear as impracticable. In the meanwhile, however, your assist-ants will have learnt that thirty seconds is quite a long time. To anyone who has ever handled a live grenade it is obvious that even four seconds can seem eternal. And once this lesson has been learnt it is never forgotten. The danger in war is to learn it too well, as the grenade in-structor is apt to do, blowing his head off while giving his fiftieth demonstration. There is no comparable risk in time of peace, so you can safely introduce the odd minute, impressing on all that time is money and that this is as true of minutes as of hours.

For years the habit of punctuality will give you a negative advantage such as the tennis player enjoys who will never double fault. But the day will come when punctuality is its own reward. The crucial decision is to be reached at this afternoon's meeting. Clutterbuck's scheme, which you deplore, is coming up again, backed by the idiotic Binworthy. The chairman rings up from a place two hundred miles away. 'I'm sorry to tell you that I have missed my 'plane. There is no other until 1.45. I am bound, therefore, to be late for the meeting. Will you take the chair until I arrive? Get Dunderidge to show you the agenda. With luck I should be there by 3.15. See you then! Good-bye.' Rubbing your hands, you will send for young Dunderidge. 'Is this the *draft* agenda? Thank you. I see there will have to be a few changes. Item 5 had better replace Item 3 and Item 3 come after Item 8. Here are new Items 9 and 10. Otherwise—yes, that will be fine. What's that? Some members have *seen* the agenda? Oh, no they haven't. They have seen it merely in *draft*. However, it doesn't matter, there being no change in the major items for discussion. Have the agenda typed now for circulation at the meeting. Yes, that's all. Don't stutter, man. Just get on with it!'

At 2.30 precisely you will be calling the meeting to order. There will be some shuffling and whispering and Garbage will come up with his protest.

GARBAGE: Not all members are present, Mr Chairman. I feel that we should defer important business until there is a full attendance.

ACTING-CHAIRMAN: But all members, Mr Garbage, have received a notice of the meeting. I have one copy of that notice before me. It reads, I quote, 2.30 p.m. It is now 2.31 and the meeting has therefore begun. Item 1: There have been no amendments proposed so I shall take it the minutes are approved. Item 2: Matters arising?

GARBAGE: Can we be told what action has been taken as a result of the decision reached under Item 7 at the last meeting?

ACTING-CHAIRMAN: That matter will be dealt with under Item 9. Any other matters arising?

GARBAGE: Has the secretary received any reply to the letter he wrote as instructed by the Committee—consequent, I mean, on the line we agreed to adopt after discussion on Item 8?

ACTING-CHAIRMAN: Look at your agenda. That reply will come up under Item 10. Any other matters arising? Very well then. Item 3. Proposals laid before this Committee in accordance with the recommendation of the Clutterbuck Report.

GARBAGE: I emphatically protest, Mr Chairman, at this attempt to deal with this important matter in the absence of Mr Binworthy, who has been closely associated with these proposals.

ACTING-CHAIRMAN: I cannot accept your view that Item 3, now under discussion, is of especial importance. All the items are important—that is why they have been placed on the agenda. And some would give priority, if any, to Item 5 or Item 7. As for any member's absence, it presumably reflects that member's opinion of this Committee and its work. I feel particularly indebted to those who thought it their duty to be present. Item 3: We have had lengthy discussions on this matter at two previous meetings, that held on March 25th and again at the meeting of May 11th. At the first we called for further information, which was afterwards provided. At the second we agreed to defer the matter until the financial position was better defined. We now know what that position is. This matter cannot be deferred for ever and I feel that the matter should be decided now. What we do not want, however, is to hear a repetition of all the arguments already used. I propose, therefore, to rule all such repetitions out of order. I shall assume that we have all heard the old arguments. Only new arguments are now admissible. Within these limits the question is now open to debate.

GARBAGE: I move that the Committee accept, in principle, the recommendations contained in the Clutterbuck Report.

ACTING-CHAIRMAN: Is that seconded?

FIDDLING: I second that.

ACTING-CHAIRMAN: Mr Tuffleigh?

TUFFLEIGH: I move, in amendment, that we add to the motion the words 'provided that no resulting expense fall on this organization'.

MR STOPWELL: I second the amendment.

GARBAGE: I submit, Mr Chairman, that this is not an amendment. It negatives the motion.

TUFFLEIGH: Not at all, sir. I am agreeing with the

motion, provided only that funds come from some other source.

ACTING-CHAIRMAN: The amendment is in order. Do you wish to speak to the amendment, Mr Tuffleigh?

TUFFLEIGH: Only to say this, Mr Chairman, that our financial position does not justify expenditure on this scheme.

ACTING-CHAIRMAN: Mr Garbage.

GARBAGE: Mr Chairman, this is monstrous! The Clutterbuck Report is perhaps the most enlightened document ever laid before us. In it we are presented with a long-term development scheme and one which——

ACTING-CHAIRMAN: You must speak to the amendment, Mr Garbage, in which the value of the scheme is not called in question. Do we have the money to spare?

GARBAGE: I would ask, rather, whether we can afford to hold back. Consider the advantages of——

ACTING-CHAIRMAN: We considered them on March 25th. They were fully outlined by Mr Binworthy.

GARBAGE: Consider then the criticism we shall incur— and indeed merit—if these proposals were to be abandoned.

ACTING-CHAIRMAN: This was fully considered on May 11th.

GARBAGE: I protest against the way in which this vital matter is being handled.

ACTING-CHAIRMAN: Your protest will be placed on record. Has anyone anything further to say? We can pro-

ceed then to vote on the amendment. Those in favour?
Three. Those against? Two. The amendment is carried.
We can proceed now to the substantive motion. Does anyone wish to speak on this? No? Then we can proceed to
vote on Mr Garbage's motion. Those in favour? Five.
Those against? None. Carried unanimously. Item 4. New
contract for the supply of stationery. You will recall, gentlemen, that we called for fresh tenders. Of these the most
economical would appear to be that submitted by Keen-
leigh and Cutting. A question arises, however, about
quality. Mr Stopwell?

STOPWELL: Well, sir, I have examined samples of——
(*Enter Binworthy and Dumpish.*)

BINWORTHY: I must apologize, Mr Chairman, for being
late. A traffic hold-up.

ACTING-CHAIRMAN: (*Blandly*) Not at all. It is very
good of you to spare the time. We are discussing Item 4.
Supply of office stationery. Mr Stopwell?

STOPWELL: I have examined samples, as I was saying
. . . (*he goes into details*) I recommend, therefore, accepting
the tender of Messrs Middling and Mugwell.

BINWORTHY: On a point of order, Mr Chairman, has
Item 5 been dealt with?

ACTING-CHAIRMAN: No, Mr Binworthy. It comes *after*
Item 4, which we are now discussing.

BINWORTHY: But the Clutterbuck Report . . .?

ACTING-CHAIRMAN: (*Gently*) Item 3? That comes
before Item 4.

BINWORTHY: It was decided, you mean, *in my absence*, and that of Mr Dumpish?

ACTING-CHAIRMAN: (*Caressingly*) Your point of view was ably represented by Mr Garbage. You will be glad to hear that his motion was carried unanimously. Item 4, Mr Stopwell?

STOPWELL: I advise, sir, accepting the tender of Messrs Middling and Mugwell.

ACTING-CHAIRMAN: Is that agreed? Thank you. Item 5. Staff Welfare Scheme. Memorandum 'C', attached to the agenda and previously circulated. Mr Dumpish?

DUMPISH: The improvements I wish to urge in Staff Welfare are summarized on page 32. I shall take them, if I may, in order.... (*Enter Chairman hastily. Acting-Chairman vacates chair.*)

CHAIRMAN: I do apologize, gentlemen, for being so late. I missed the aircraft which would have brought me here in time. I can honestly claim that this is, with me, a very rare occurrence. I am usually the most punctual of men, having been taught in early life that business depends upon being in time. Yes, gentlemen, as I always say, *Punctuosity Pays*!

ALL: Hear, hear!

CHAIRMANITY

To be present and properly briefed when the meeting begins is the first rule but not the only one. In order to rise in the world through clever committee work, filling in turn the offices of Secretary, Vice-Chairman and Chairman, you need a full knowledge of how committees work, expand and ramify. The study of this subject is known today as Comitology. And while it should never be your object to become too involved in a merely academic research, you will do well to master the elements of this subject. More than that, you should follow the current trends of thought and know, at least in outline, what the most recent discoveries are. Comitology is attracting world-wide interest and few indeed can afford to ignore what has been achieved in this, the latest of the biological sciences.

Work has centred, as we all know, on the Institute of Comitology, the main building of which was developed on a site between Waterloo Station and County Hall. There it has been found convenient to distribute research projects between departments specializing respectively in History, Evolution, Current and Future Developments, Comparative Chairmanity, Pathetic Honsecticism and International Comitology. For a full account of all that is being done in this field the reader should refer to *Theoretical and Applied Comitology, an Interim Report* edited by Peering-Snooperton and published by the Oxford University Press, in three volumes, in 1960. Here there is space for only the most fleeting and desultory comment, a mere random illustration of all that is being attempted. An early discovery in the History Department, for example, was that the word 'Committee' was originally singular, the term being applied to:

> . . . a person charged to represent the interests of a lunatic. Committees are appointed for those lunatics only whose mental incapacity has been established.
> —*Palgrave's Dictionary of Political Economy*

As lunatics became steadily more numerous, it was logical to increase their representatives from one to three, so that the word 'Committee' has become (like House of Commons and Den of Thieves) a noun of multitude. It is in this form that the Committee is conceived; and the birth—when the Committee, as we know it, is actually formed—is of a body comprising three to five members. It is certain now that the *embryonic* committee numbers three and cannot well be less. Without that initial number it is impossible to elect a chairman, appoint a secretary and have any committee left. And with three actually present, effective work can be done. But what if a member, what if even two members, should be absent? It is to allow for this possibility that the first extension of membership occurs, the arguments used all centring upon the difficulty of assembling a quorum.

The classic form is thus undoubtedly a Committee of five with a quorum of three. In the Institute's Department of Evolution the problems of growth and expansion are studied under the microscope. Once the problem of attendance has been temporarily solved by enlarging the Committee and allowing a wider margin for absenteeism, the process of expansion has fairly begun. The Committee grows and swells, throws out sub-committees and extends its laden branches. It flourishes and blossoms, sunlit on top and shady beneath, the loftiness of its public motions contrasting oddly with the wormlike activities which go on beneath the ground. In due course, finally, it decays and dies, scattering the seed from which other committees will spring. Familiar to the evolutionary Comitologist is the whole course of nature from seed to harvest. There is certainly no lack of material for study. Papers read at the Institute's recent International Conference shed light, for example, on the Committee of Public Safety, the Committee for Reciprocity Information, the Committee on Interpretation of the Nation-wide Marine Definitions and (above all, towering in status) the American Committee for Flags of Necessity. By mentioning but a few of these great examples, we bring to mind the whole biological cycle from conception to adultery, from senility to death.

The basic principles of Comitology have been discovered in the Institute's Department of Evolution. Present and Future trends have been described and foretold in the papers which emanate from the Department of Current and Future Developments. It is clear, nevertheless, that the most sensational progress has been in the two related fields of Comparative Chairmanity and Pathetic Honsecticism. In broad outline at least, the results of this research should be more widely known.

Students of Comparative Chairmanity have agreed to classify their work under four general headings: (I) Inanimism, (II) Blahmanism, (III) Browbeatnicism, and (IV) Confusionism. They assume that it is the object of every

95

chairman to have his own way with the minimum of effort. Chairmen are classified, therefore, on the basis of the methods they use.

Taking these methods in order, the technique of the Inanimist is to prevent the discussion becoming animated. He aims at creating a dull and deadening atmosphere in which nothing seems to matter. His simplest and probably his best trick is to be partly or totally deaf.

'Item 7. Application from Mr Needham-Baddeley for an increase of emoluments. May I take it that this application is rejected?'

'Well, Mr Chairman, it does seem to me that——'

'Any comments? No? Very well, then. The Application is refused. Item 8 . . .'

Only a bold man with an exceptionally loud voice can attract the Chairman's attention or make it clear that Item 7 is still under discussion. There are several other ways of stifling argument and the devout Inanimist will know them all.

The Blahman achieves the same result by different means. The essence of his technique is to blind the committee with science. Facts and figures are quoted rapidly, graphs are fluttered and put aside, diagrams are waved and charts briefly displayed, technicalities mentioned and knowledge assumed. The committee is swamped by a flood of percentages and basic trends, the members being still floundering and befogged when the meeting is adjourned. Blahmanism is common today in all fields of activity, but reaches its mystic heights among people concerned with education. The leading exponents of blahmanism are not

D

and never have been teachers. They are merely educationalizers, the carrion-seeking vultures who hover over the schools at various heights but with a common rapacity. They deal in purely theoretical concepts as applied to purely hypothetical pupils, but they shine in Committee. A chairman of this type will introduce Item 14 with a little speech on these lines:

'Item 14. Report from the Sub-Committee appointed to consider Dr Fogwell's Interim Recommendations, with enclosures A to K and copies of relevant correspondence number I to XVII. This report, which we have all read with interest, makes it clear that achievement batteries did not, in this instance, give us as consistent a result as the ergograph test—least of all with the cerebrotonic (as opposed to the visceratonic and somatonic) pupils, a high percentage of these proving too extratensive to fit into the Behavioural Pattern as produced from the interquartile range and measured by the Second Stanford-Binel Testing. The statistical results are summarized at appendix XXXIV, and illustrated in the chart placed opposite page 79. From this you can see the percentile curve for yourselves, from which (I would suggest) only one conclusion can be drawn. Is this a case, you will ask, of the Muller-Lyer Illusion? Should we have applied the Child Rorschach Responses—at least in the atypical or ambiequal cases? I think myself that we should have been wrong to do that. Our initial classification in the endomorphic, mesomorphic and ectomorphic scales gives us, surely, sufficient data upon which to base our Octogenesis of Child Behaviour. I might add that the jagged histogram offers as meaningful evidence as the Coefficient of Colligation. With the evidence so incontrovertible, I assume that we shall accept the Sub-Committee's Report, with recommendations 1 to 8? Thank you. We pass now to Item 15.'

The other members of the Committee have no idea, of course, what all this drivel is supposed to be about. Glimpsing successive columns of figures, equations and graphs, they are too numbed and bewildered to demand an explanation. Nor would it help them if they did, for the explanation would be just as obscure as the thing to be explained.

'Ah!' the Chairman would say. 'But Atomism and Behaviourism are not synonymous. Neither, for that matter, are Atomism and Wholism fundamentally opposed. So we are brought back, surely, to the same conclusion?' Knowing what the result would be the committee members say nothing, ask nothing and dumbly acquiesce in everything. They seldom realize that any remedy exists. In point of fact, however, the Blahmanist can be foiled by Blahmanism. Another Blahman on the committee can riposte smartly with another consignment of Blah.

With Blah meeting Blah in head-on collision, the other committee members will be more befogged than ever. But they will probably vote against the Chairman if given the chance. For Blahmanism the remedy exists. Can the same be said of Browbeatnicism? It is more than doubtful. The Browbeatnik Chairman is the bullying bulldozer, the red-faced loud-voiced man who seems on the point of apoplexy when opposed. Essence of his technique is to state or imply that the matter has been decided already, the issue not seriously in question.

'We are virtually committed to this scheme by our resolution under Item 4 taken at the last meeting.'

'But, surely, Mr Chairman, we resolved merely to ask Snatching & Wriggle to submit a rough design.'

'It is late in the day to go back on our decision. Much work has been done. They could sue us for the fee payable in respect of an abandoned scheme. Then we should have to call in another firm with inevitable delay.'

'But they were only to do a sketch and a preliminary estimate.'

'I should say that we are committed to this scheme and to these architects. May I take that as agreed?'

'I submit, sir, that you were not empowered to commit us.'

'So you are suggesting that I exceeded my brief?'

'No, sir. I merely say that we are not yet committed to this particular scheme.'

'Do you question my INTEGRITY?'

'I have said nothing about your integrity.'

'You practically accuse me of dishonesty.'

'No, sir, I do not.'

'The question is whether I have the confidence of this committee or not. (*Shouts.*) Am I still Chairman? (*Screams.*) *Is my integrity in doubt?* AM I TO BE INSULTED BY EVERY NEWLY JOINED MEMBER??? (*Murmured indications of confidence.*) Very well, then, I must ask Mr Barwell to withdraw his allegations.'

'I made no allegation, Mr Chairman.'

'I accept your apology. I hope we can now return to business. Having committed ourselves to the scheme which is laid before us today it remains only to decide on certain priorities. Two directors of Snatching &

Wriggle are in attendance and I propose now to call them in.'

In Browbeatnik tactics an important part is played by the word 'integrity' which is very commonly used by crooks. Once the objector has been made to seem a critic of the Chairman's honesty, the other members feel bound to register sympathy, which can then be accepted as support for the policy the chairman is advocating. All objections are then swept aside and some hideous building is the result.

In the field of Comparative Chairmanity, Confusionism is not a recent development. Only during the last two years, however, has there been any systematic study of its prevalence, application and effect. The Confusionist Chairman allows the meeting to lapse into chaos, no one knowing what exactly is being discussed or even around what item on the Agenda the disagreement has arisen. Everyone is speaking at once, no two of the speakers on the same subject and few on topics that are even vaguely related. The resulting babel sounds something like this:

. . . But really this new parking scheme seems impossibly complicated. . . . I have nothing against depth advertising but I question whether we have gone to the right firm. Why Hydden Pearce, Waders, Ltd? Why them in particular . . .? If we *have* to change the auditors, then Messrs Redynk & Blew, Ltd, are the inevitable choice—no one would dispute that. . . . But why admit only blue stickers after 9.0 . . .? And this is the very type of campaign that might boomerang—virtually a plan to advertise what we can't supply. . . . Our previous auditors were too slow

—that is generally agreed—but gave good service and knew the business backwards. . . . And what are the people with white stickers to do—sell their cars and walk . . .? Frankly, I distrust this Company. . . . You can't be serious! Redynk & Blew, Ltd, are among the oldest and most respected firms in town. You will find them excellent. You can't go wrong with Blew. . . . That's all very well for those with blue stickers. My concern is for those with *white*. . . . I don't know what you mean. Whyte's advertising bureau is not under discussion. Now, Pearce is known to me personally. I say nothing against him, mind you. But there is such a thing as being too clever. . . . Too clever? I never before heard it suggested that our old auditors were too *clever*. Too hidebound, perhaps. Too old-fashioned, maybe. But too *clever*? Their trouble was that they wanted everything in black and white. . . . But that would be impracticable! To have all stickers in Black and White would make it impossible for the men on the gate. They have difficulty enough as it is—the colours are none too distinguishable at night. . . . That is exactly what these advertising experts seem unable to learn. . . . That is just it. The old auditors couldn't adjust themselves. . . . Why should the park attendants adjust themselves . . .? I have heard that these people were quite recently in the red. . . . What, Redynks? You must be confusing them with another firm. They have never been in the red. . . . It is not the red stickers we are discussing—they are confined to the Directors, who have their own parking place. We don't have to worry about *them*. . . . But I *do* worry about them. They will give the public the wrong impression. . . . Think of the lime that is tossed. . . . Advertising space. . . . Audited accounts. . . . Parking lot. . . . Lot of P.R.

accounts.... Accounts of accident.... Accidental error....
Error to publicize. . . . Public scandal. . . . Scandalous
delay. . . . Delay in printing. . . . Printing of stickers. . . .
Sticklers for etiquette. . . . A ticket for offending. . . .
Fending off inquiry. . . . Inquiry into P.R. . . . Peering in
the dark. . . . Dark suspicions. . . . Musicians? . . . No,
suspicions.... Of what?

While the babel becomes more noisy and the confusion
more confused the Chairman smiles benignly, interjecting
an occasional question—'Are you speaking for or against
the amendment?'—or putting in some acid comment—
'Really, I question whether these remarks should be
minuted'—so adding further obscurity to what is already
obscure enough. After twenty-five minutes of babble and
uproar the members will pause for breath. And at that
moment the Chairman suddenly bangs his hammer on the
table. Amidst the breathless silence that ensues, he pro-
claims the sense of the meeting. 'Well, we are all agreed on
that item of the Agenda. I propose, therefore, to move on
to the next. This is a matter of some complexity, arising
from a previous decision of the Committee, which I propose to consider somewhat out of sequence and about
which there has already been some informal discussion.
Mr Blatherwick, I understand that you have something to
say on this matter?' There is fresh uproar, lasting this time
for fifteen minutes, at the end of which the Chairman says:
'Thank you. With that item disposed of, we can now proceed to another. . . .' After some two hours of this, the
Chairman brings the meeting to an end. 'That concludes
the Agenda. Any other business? The meeting is adjourned.' A few days later, the members receive copies of

the neatly tabulated minutes recording the Chairman's decision on each item. 'The Secretary does a wonderful job,' they tell each other, 'to make sense of it all.'

While some chairmen are content with having their own way, others want their dictatorship to be generally known. It is one of the paradoxes of Comitology that, whereas the object of a Committee may be to save one individual from the responsibility of making an unpopular decision, the Chairman will sometimes claim all responsibility for the decisions made. This is particularly true of any public inquiry and the process begins with the Committee's official description. It is initially worded something like this:

> A Special Committee Of Inquiry set up by Royal Command to enquire into the Causes of Juvenile Delinquency, its prevalence at different periods and in different Counties, its cost to the public and to the schools, and the measures so far taken to deal with it; as also to recommend such future legislation as may tend, in the Committee's Opinion, to mitigate and eventually abolish the evils resulting therefrom.

With such a title as this, there is little likelihood of the Committee being referred to except in an abbreviated form of words. Such a body as this would probably be called the Juvenile Delinquency Committee. It is the object, therefore, of Mr Leverage, the intended Chairman (should he seek publicity), to confuse this title in advance. This is best done by adding further and disconnected objects of inquiry. The wording might be amended to read: 'to inquire into the causes of illegal activity among children, adolescents, the feeble-minded and senile with special reference to drug-addiction, pornography and blackmail, not to mention incest, mayhem and suicide, their prevalence. . . . etc.' By thus extending and confusing the object of the exercise, adding doubt as to whether incest is included or specifically ruled out, the newspapers are prevented from referring to the Juvenile Delinquency Committee. They have no alternative but to call it the Leverage Committee, from which will eventually come the Leverage Report. The Chairman will thus have all the publicity to himself.

Closely connected with Comitology is a new subject for investigation called Subcomitology; the study of the Sub-Committee. There has been some controversy over this, some doubt as to whether the subject exists. 'What is Subcomitology?' asked one of our leading authorities. 'It is merely Comitology as studied by the sub-normal.' Another scholar asked, 'But is Subcomitology a Discipline?' Whether we approve or not, however, Subcomitology has come to stay. And, if only for that reason, the controversy that has arisen must be thought deplorable. There should be co-operation rather than rivalry between social scientists whose work is so nearly allied. For while the science of Subcomitology most certainly exists, it cannot be divorced from Comitology as a whole. We must remember, in this connection, that one function of the Sub-Committee is to defeat a rival group on the Committee of which the Sub-Committee is an offshoot. The party headed by A is thwarted in its honest endeavours by the faction which centres on B. It is natural, therefore, that A should propose to split up the detailed work among four sub-committees. When this is agreed he will naturally contrive to delegate all the important work to the sub-committee of which he proposes to make himself the chairman and in which his supporters will have a majority.

The B-minded people will dominate another sub-committee under B's chairmanship; one which is given an impressive title but nothing of significance to transact. This normal and everyday procedure involves the use of sub-committees as a constitutional device but is one phase, essentially, in the struggle for power as between A and B. How can we say, therefore, that the Comitologist can ignore this sort of manœuvre, leaving it for the Subcomitologist to investigate? Here, surely, is a case for co-operation.

Should we agree that Subcomitology exists as distinct from Comitology but as a subject very closely allied, what are we to say of Infrasubcomitology? This is the study of the sub-sub-committees which the sub-committee will often project; a study to which some research departments are nowadays wholly devoted. Is there a case for a specialization as specialized as this? No, there is not. This is the point at which common sense must intervene. To talk of Infrasubcomitology and of Subinfrasubcomitological Studies is to go a great deal too far, more especially in a university context. Professors need to be continually reminded that their work must centre on the basic academic disciplines, and that specialization, beyond a certain point, becomes absurd.

From even as brief an outline as this it will be apparent that our knowlege of Comitology, both Pure and Applied, is steadily increasing; as is also, of course, the number of Committees available for study. It would be idle to pretend that this multiplication of committees is regarded with equal satisfaction by all. An influential group of those wives who have come to describe themselves as gas-widows went so far recently as to announce the discovery of an Eleventh Commandment: 'Thou shalt not Commit.' There can be no general sympathy, however, with so reactionary a point of view. The machinery of administration must continue to function and the study of this machinery must continue to present us with a subject for scientific investigation, as also with a career for those who cannot think what else to do. To paraphrase a wise remark made by His Royal Highness the Duke of Edinburgh, what is the use of man if science does not survive?

FUNCTION OF FOLLY

By astute work in committee, by a knowledge of Comitology (both theoretical and applied) you have risen to a position of trust. If no disaster occurs you will gradually gain the reputation of a Man of Ability. You will be a man in whom others have learnt to place their confidence. With your own position thus established, you will begin to observe with surprise the incompetence of others. The apparent folly of some will make you wonder whether they can be of any use to the organization. Is there any purpose they can serve? Pondering on this problem, as well you may, you will come to ask yourself the fundamental questions about skill and ability. What are these qualities and how do they differ from each other? How do mediocre executives achieve promotion? And is disaster the invariable result?

To begin with, what is skill? Skill is the capacity to do something which is not particularly easy. Ability is the capacity to get things done, mainly through the effort and skill of other people. The violinist has skill, the conductor has to have ability as well. And ability is always in fairly short supply. It does not command the famine price of genius but it is always scarce and often unobtainable. Such is the nature of ability, however, that it often passes unnoticed. It seems quite normal, to most people, that a complex organization should run smoothly, its output steadily improving, its staff contented and its costs held down. But there is nothing normal about it. It is about as natural as a beautiful lawn, cut and rolled, with weeds eliminated and worms removed. No such lawn will happen by itself. It is the result of an initial effort and continual care, and neither weeds nor worms will go of their own accord. Somewhere in the organization's centre there will be the man responsible. Into his office will pass a sporadic procession of people who are worried, baffled or aggrieved. Out of his office will come a procession of people whose minds have been set at rest. They may not be happy but they need no longer worry. They know at least what the decision is to be.

'What am I to do with young Crabtree? He does nothing but grumble and complain.'

'That is because he has too little to do. I shall transfer him next week to the transport department.'

'Connie is always going sick. Should we get rid of her?'

'No. Her trouble is that her boy-friend, George, is on a public-relations course. He will be back in ten days.'

'What are we to do with Blackie's team while No. 7 Plant is being overhauled?'

'For one week they will do maintenance work on No. 3, after which they can have three days' holiday.'

'Sam Deadweed is asking for his old job back, having heard it will be vacant.'

'It will be vacant in October. But, Sam? No. Tell him there are jobs going at Frittering and Muddle's chemical plant.'

'We have an application from Tom Wormley, who used to work in the packing shed.'

'No.'

'Old Bedrock is having one of his fits of depression.'

'So I hear. We'll send him to represent the Group at the Harrogate Conference.

'Phil Feverish is asking for promotion.'

'He can't have it. But tell him to be at my office to-morrow at 10.0.'

'There's been a theft of £200 from the petty cash!'

'Close all doors and all the outer gates. Tell the security chief to meet me in the Board Room in three minutes' time.'

'Please sir, I feel unwell.'

'Drink this. Lie down for ten minutes and then go home. Make up for lost time tomorrow.'

'I beg to offer my resignation.'

'It is not accepted. Take tomorrow off. Play golf over the week-end. See me again on Monday at 9.30.'

Here is ability at work and the final result is to be measured as much by the things that don't happen as by the things that do. The factory is not burnt down. The workers do not go on strike. Bill does not resign and Betty does not commit suicide. For all this the Manager receives little credit, for things that don't happen are hard to assess. There is no proof, to begin with, that disaster had ever been imminent. But, whether appreciated or not, the ability is there. Fortunate is the organization of which this can be said.

In the imaginary dialogue quoted above the essence of the ability shown is in the Manager's attitude towards each problem. He decides in each case what to do next. He wastes not a minute on what has already been done. The trademark of incompetence, by contrast, is apparent from an attitude which is exactly the opposite. It is again best illustrated in dialogue:

'There has been a serious accident in the foundry. One of the men is pinned under a machine.'

'Who was in charge? Joe Wittering? It would be! Why did we ever hire that man?'

'The foundations have cracked in the new workshop—one wall may collapse at any moment.'

'Well, don't blame *me*. Lashup and Buttering were the engineers. I never thought much of them.'

'We have proof of a communist cell organized among the electricians.'

'What has the Personnel Department been playing at? Do they expect me to do their work for them?'

'We have lost the Oldrope Contract.'

'I *knew* that would happen. If only that last delivery had been on time!'

'Our output has fallen again this month.'

'Not *again*? It's all the fault of the efficiency experts. We should never have called them in!'

The reaction of incompetence is always the same and the sequence is as follows: I am not the person responsible. Whose fault is it? Why did we (or you, or they—never 'I') make this mistake in the past, cause of the present mishap? If only we hadn't! Why doesn't someone own up? Why didn't someone do something? Why did I ever accept this job? From all this gibbering there emerges no word of guidance as to what anyone is to do *next*.

Ability, as contrasted with ineptitude, is relatively scarce. Nor is there any certainty that it will be used even where available. Organizations with every precaution against waste of time and money will often waste ability. One result of this is the preferment of the incompetent, which is to some extent inevitable. Where in fact avoidable, it comes about through the rejection of every candidate against whom anything can be said. A is proposed but he is said to be arty, B is suggested but he is too bold. C's name is mentioned but he is too hearty, D's dictatorial, E is too old. What about F? He is frankly too charming. And what about G? Gossip says he's a queer. As for old H, he is much too alarming; and K—we must face it—drinks far too much beer. How if we settle for L? But he's ailing. M is too deaf, or so we hear tell. Forget about N—why, his memory's failing! And that goes for O, who argues too well. Shall we have P? Too caustic and clever. Q is too quiet and R is too rude. S is so silent and T talks for ever. U is efficient but horribly crude. And V? Irreplaceable! Capable! Valuable! Really *too* valuable just where he is. But W? W? He'll never trouble you. Let's turn him down and return to the Quiz. Come now to X—does anyone know him? What does he look like? We can't just recall. He can't be too fat or we'd surely have noticed. He can't be too short and he can't be too tall. He can't be too stupid. He can't be too brilliant, for no one remembers a word that he said. Is he hardworking and is he resilient? Perhaps he is neither. Perhaps he is dead. To X no one can offer the slightest objection. We are none of us sure that we know him by sight. He gives rise to no jealousy, hate or affection. Appoint him at once! For this post he is right!

So X, the nonentity, is appointed. Should he thus reach the chief executive position, the result is likely to be fatal. If, however, he is merely No 2, the situation may develop in one of several ways. Much depends, to begin with, on the quality of his negation. It often happens that the man who is negative in all other respects will conceal a positive and smouldering dislike of all those superior to him in brains, initiative, imagination and drive; which necessarily means hating practically everyone. This is the origin, as we all know, of Injelititis; that dread disease to which so many institutions succumb. But his negation may be too complete to admit of jealousy, his self-satisfaction being such as to make him the intellectual superior (in his own opinion) of everyone he meets. Where that is the case, Injelititis will never occur. It is undeniable, on the other hand, that the organization may suffer in other ways. Much could be written on this subject but our present object is different. For the stupidity of a high executive can, in some instances, prove useful. It is even postulated by some authorities that a measure of stupidity is actually essential. While we may not go quite as far as that, we cannot deny that stupidity, in some forms and in some circumstances, may well have its value. Its use depends, however, on the negation being less complete than the stupidity. Let us assume, to illustrate this point, that the new No. 2 has been purely negative up to the time of his appointment. He has made no mistakes, aroused no hostilities, done nothing in fact of any kind. But he is forced now to decide on occasion between this and that. If his negation is complete and his stupidity mixed with a little cunning he will refer each decision to someone else. But he may lose something of his negation as a result of his promotion, in which case he will try to decide. With average stupidity, his decisions will mostly be wrong. But with *absolute* stupidity they will *all* be wrong. And that is the point at which the man thought useless can suddenly become invaluable.

In a few organizations there is to be found a man who is always right. 'No,' he says quietly, 'that scheme is too complex. It won't work.' And that is where the discussion ends. Such a man has the sort of authority, on a higher level, that Old Dick has in matters less abstruse. We all know Dick. The problem is one, let us say, of grading a consignment of raw cotton. There are two ways of doing this. One way is to submit a sample to the works laboratory. The other and quicker way is to send for Dick. By the first method a prolonged series of scientific tests will provide a formula which will lead in turn to a provisional conclusion. By the second method, Dick handles the stuff for five seconds and gives his verdict 'Second Grade'. And Second Grade it is. Heaven forbid that we should regard the laboratory test as useless (for Dick, some day, will retire) but no one would dream of disputing what Dick says. Almost as final is the verdict of that rare executive, the man who is always right. In any discussion on policy, views will be advanced and disputed, modified and opposed. Then, often enough when all present are tired of arguing, the quiet man in the corner takes his pipe out of his mouth and speaks for the first time. 'I think we shall have to defer this decision until we hear from Wainwright.' For the moment, he seems to speak with the authority of the ages, representing the accumulated wisdom of mankind. What he says is final. In many an organization this sage conclusion may come from one of several. In others it comes nearly always from the one; the man who is always right.

In theory, the man who is always right (where he exists) should be made the chief executive; as does occasionally happen. But he is often, in practice, too unpopular. From the point of view of his own ambition, he would do well to be wrong on every tenth occasion just to keep the rest in countenance. Failing that precaution, his unpopularity has its origin in the occasions when he has been outvoted and overruled. 'Do that,' he has said, 'and you will lose the Berheimer account.' They do it and the account is lost. He never says 'I told you so!' He never refers to the matter again. But the others remember it against him just as if his prediction had been the cause of the loss. Just as people never forgive the man they have injured, neither do they readily forgive the man whose good advice they have agreed to reject. He becomes a shade less popular on each occasion; as happens to the man who correctly predicts the coming storm. So there is not, of necessity, any great future for the man who is always right. There is not, of necessity, a great future for the man with ability of any kind. Fortunate, however, is the organization in which there is someone whose instinctive verdict is so infallible. While it may do him no good, it is extremely useful to others. They have a compass, whether they look at it or not.

But the man who is always right is something of a rarity. In the more average organization there are differing opinions among people who are each of them right for much of the time. A wants to accept the lowest tender. B thinks that this would lead to higher cost in the end. C is undecided and D is sick. What is E to do? Failing a man who is always right, what if the organization contains a man who is always wrong? This brings us back to X, the newly appointed No. 2, whose stupidity, since promotion, has become more prominent than his previous nonentity. Why not ask him and then do the opposite? Where it is a simple choice between alternatives 1 and 2, this method may be infallible. Where the alternatives are three, it may serve to eliminate one of them. The system has obvious possibilities. It must depend, however, on X being consistently wrong. For him to be merely 75 per cent wrong is not good enough. So that the appointment of X (Mr Cypher, to use his full name) should lead at once to a scientific test of his reversed infallibility. This is done by putting problems to him which have already been solved. Mr Haywire was tried as Personnel Manager and resigned at the end of six weeks, having reduced that department to chaos. Advertisement 113 was used and led to a 23 per cent reduction in sales. A finance scheme was tried and proved wildly successful up to the point when it was declared illegal. The strike which threatened last year was instigated by Mark Cyst, a welder, but abandoned owing to the sturdy opposition of John Playfair, who drives the works' locomotive. It is on these problems (of which he has no inside knowledge) that Mr Cypher will be tested.

MAINSTAY: Should Mr Makepeace leave us (as I am told he may—but this is in strict confidence) we shall need a new Personnel Manager. Various names have been suggested, that of Mr Haywire included. Have we any views on his suitability? Bob?

BOB BEDROCK: I think he would be worth trying. A painstaking, methodical man—quiet but popular. Yes, I think he might be a success.

KEN KINGPOST: I'm sorry but I don't agree. Haywire seems to me too vague and scatterbrained. He might fail completely.

MAINSTAY: Mr Cypher?

CYPHER: Well, I have known Haywire for a few months only. But he impresses me as a very responsible man. Very respectful and ready to accept advice. Yes, I think highly of Haywire. I don't see how we could find anyone better.

MAINSTAY: Thank you. We have now to consider a new advertisement for our chief product. Copies are before us. What do you think of it?

KINGPOST: Very striking indeed. No risk of it not being noticed. A clever design with a telling slogan. It should be a great success.

BEDROCK: I wonder? It could backfire. The trademark looks too much like a swastika. One of the figures shown might offend the Labour Party and the wording would certainly offend the Cavalry Club.

MAINSTAY: Mr Cypher?

CYPHER: I agree with Kingpost. It has all the qualities we need to project our public image. I think these dangers are imaginary.

After Cypher has proved equally wrong on the Share Incentive Scheme the testing process becomes exciting. To be wrong on one issue is normal. To be wrong on two is not exceptional. To be wrong on three, however, is more than a coincidence, and thenceforward the results become conclusive.

MAINSTAY: Our next problem concerns Mr Mark Cyst, our Chief Welder; a man known to most of us as a shop steward, very active in union affairs. He is also a skilled and experienced technician. We learn that he has been offered a similar job but with higher pay at Messrs Bonehead & Nitwit's No. 13 Division. Are we to equal their offer so as to retain him? Ken?

KINGPOST: Well, he certainly knows his job. It is a question whether we can find another man equally skilled. Nor, if we did, would his pay be much less than Cyst is asking. I think we should meet his demands.

BEDROCK: I'm not sure that we should make any special effort to keep him. His union activities have been unhelpful and even obstructive. I should let him go.

CYPHER: I agree with Mr Kingpost. Skilled technicians are not easy to find. Cyst is an intelligent man—I've noticed that—and quite well educated. He should be a good influence in the union. I think we should make an effort to keep him. (*The others exchange significant glances.*)

MAINSTAY: We have a rather similar problem with Playfair, the locomotive driver. He too has been offered better pay elsewhere and he too has been active in union politics. Is he worth a raise—or not? Bob?

BEDROCK: Well, we must admit that he has done well. His maintenance standards have been high. We have had no accidents in shunting. He has never grumbled about working overtime. So I think he deserves a raise.

KINGPOST: That's all very well, but drivers are fairly easy to find. We should receive half a dozen applications for his job and two or three from men with experience.

Why not replace Playfair with a younger man, whose pay could be actually less?

MAINSTAY: Mr Cypher?

CYPHER: I think we should let him go. Playfair is a surly and outspoken fellow. I can't think he is a good influence. Don't offer him a penny more than he is getting. Not a *penny*!

MAINSTAY: Thank you, Mr Cypher. . . .

It is fairly clear by now that Cypher is consistent. He has been wrong five times out of five. The moment has come, therefore, to apply the final test; a problem which concerns the future.

MAINSTAY: Our last question this afternoon concerns the proposal to call in a firm of business consultants. We have had lengthy discussions, as you all know, with representatives of Suckerseek, Mistery and Leech. What we have now to decide is our recommendation to the Board. Shall we ask them for a full report on our organization and method? Bob?

BEDROCK: It seems to me that we have largely committed ourselves already, having taken up so much of their time. I feel that we should go ahead now and engage them as consultants.

KINGPOST: No, Bob, we are not committed to that extent. We could pay them a small fee and say 'good-bye'. And that, I think, is what we should do. I am not greatly impressed with them as consultants.

MAINSTAY: I know, Mr Cypher, that you have another

appointment in five minutes. I hope, however, that we may have your opinion on this matter before you go?

CYPHER: Yes, I must be going. But I feel, myself, that these consultants could give us some useful advice. I was greatly impressed by their knowledge, their experience and integrity. Each of the partners had something different to offer and the firm itself is extremely well known. Their report should prove a milestone in the history of the group. I say, let's go ahead! I'll leave you now and should add that I will be very disappointed if we withdraw at this late stage of the negotiations. This is a matter in which you can safely trust my judgement! (*Exit.*)

The others look at each other with all the excitement of discovery. It seems almost too good to be true. Their quest is at an end.

MAINSTAY: So our little experiment has been a success. Five out of five!

BEDROCK: You know, I almost *like* Cypher!

KINGPOST: Well, that settles the question about those consultants. We get rid of them.

MAINSTAY: Of course. I'll ring them up at once. In fairness, they should have the earliest possible warning (*Telephones.*) Is that Suckerseek, Mistery and Leech? Who is that speaking? . . . Can I have a word with Mr Suckerseek? . . . No? . . . Mr Leech, then? . . . Really! . . . Good God! . . . Is that so? . . . Incredible! . . . But how extraordinary! . . . No bail allowed, I suppose? . . . Of course I understand . . . very good of you, officer, to tell me all this . . . Thanks . . . Quite! . . . Thanks a lot! Good-bye . . .

(*To the others*) That was a detective, left in charge of their office.

BEDROCK: But why? What happened?

MAINSTAY: They went bankrupt. Suckerseek is arrested on a charge of fraud.

KINGPOST: And the rest of them—are they all involved?

MAINSTAY: No, apparently not. Leech was held on a charge of treason.

BEDROCK: Which implicates Mistery?

MAINSTAY: Oh, no. Scotland Yard were after him for molesting little girls.

KINGPOST: So our theory about Cypher is amply confirmed!

MAINSTAY: Most dramatically confirmed. In Cypher, that invaluable man, we have reverse infallibility. He is our misleader and misguide, the mirror in which truth appears backwards. He is our compass with the needle pointing south. . . . Which reminds me—he should be leaving the Managing Director's office any moment now. (*Telephones.*) That you, Deadshot? Mainstay here. Stop all traffic in the main avenue for the next ten minutes.

KINGPOST: But *why*, Harry?

MAINSTAY: Don't you see, Ken? Cypher will have to cross the avenue to get back to his office. We simply can't afford to have an accident. . . .

PAPERWORK

Nearing the summit of your organization, a hierarchy in which you rank now perhaps as Number Three, you will begin to realize what it means to be at the top. You will be in sole charge when others are on holiday. You will see at close range how the highest executives work and you will come to realize what their difficulties are. Chief among their problems, you will find, is one with which you have been acquainted from the start; the problem of paper. But here, at the very senior level, the problem will seem to have acquired a new dimension. Paper is no longer a nuisance but has become a nightmare. More than that, it is a brooding menace, a seething tide which can swamp and drown. On your success in dealing with it your next promotion must depend. It is a flood in which you must either sink or swim.

This flood of paper which now threatens to submerge the world is something peculiar to this century. The Hellenistic scribes who wrote on papyrus, the Chinese bureaucrats who exercised their penmanship on silk, and even the eighteenth-century clerks who inscribed their civilities on rag paper with a quill pen, were guiltless of anything that could be called mass production. It is our own age that has developed the swiftness of communication, the abundance of paper, the multiplication of copies and the widespread semi-literacy which are the immediate causes of the paper flood. Ease of communication has also made practicable such a degree of centralized control as was never known before. Until a century ago every large scale and scattered organization or empire was engaged in a ceaseless struggle to make its distant units conform with central policy. For reference to headquarters there was neither the inclination nor the time. Those in positions of theoretical responsibility read with helpless dismay of provinces annexed, officials sacked, branches opened and ships sold, their bleating protests coming perpetually too late. With the laying of transoceanic cables they felt for the first time that they had their agents on the leash. From about 1875 began, therefore, that tightening of the chain that has finally destroyed the effectiveness of (among other things) colonialism and diplomacy. The professional bargaining of plenipotentiaries has given place to the bickering of impotent office boys, each tied to the apron-strings of a government which has never even heard the persuasions of the other side. Diplomatically, administratively, commercially, the process of centralization has been carried to its logical conclusion with all authority vested too often in a single man; and he, from overwork, quite obviously off his head.

It was inevitable that the central administration would make full use of the tools that had suddenly become available. After centuries of frustration those in authority could at last impose their policy upon the whole organization, not merely from day to day but from hour to hour. They could exact the fullest information, collate the most detailed returns, draw up the most voluminous directives and issue the most peremptory commands. Of these opportunities they have made the fullest use. But for all this they have had to pay the price. The penalty has been that correspondence pours on them in the present flood. Surrounding themselves with executives, they battle with a rising tide of paper. Ordinarily waist-deep in letters and memoranda, a week's illness will bring the high-water mark up to their chin. Rather than drown, the key man prefers to suppress his symptoms and stay at his desk; often with the worst results for all concerned.

After more than fifty years of tightening control, with all initiative killed at the circumference and all leisure abolished at the top, some people have begun to ask whether much that is now technically possible is, always and everywhere, practically wise. Some newly formed commercial empires, the results of mergers, have preferred to avoid centralization except for purposes of raising capital. In others, already centralized, the question is being asked whether control from the centre may not have gone too far. In a few, a very few, the machine has been actually put into reverse. One chain store organization, for example, has totally revised its system of control. Merely by deciding that the head office should trust the branch manager, that the branch manager should trust the girls behind the counter, and that the girls should trust the customers, this organization dispensed with time cards, complaint reports and stockroom forms. It was agreed to assume that all concerned are honest; partly because they are and partly because it would still be cheaper even if they were not. In thus eliminating 22,000,000 pieces of paper per year, weighing 105 tons, all that the directors lost was a mass of statistical information of which no use, in fact, had ever been made. One result was an immediate reduction of staff. Another result has been the flattering interest shown by other firms.

Here is one Board that has escaped, somehow, from the toils.

In this particular instance the time for reducing paperwork began, significantly, when the Chairman of the Board was visiting a branch store on a Saturday afternoon. Finding all the girls working overtime to complete the catalogue cards he asked what the cards were for. 'For?' repeated the supervisor blankly, 'They are for filling in. Here is one, sir. You can see for yourself that it has to be filled in.' 'But why?' asked the chairman. No one could tell him. No one knew. No one had ever known. It was from that moment that the paper-saving movement began. What we have to realize is that nothing would have begun had the Chairman stayed in his office, holding committee meetings and answering mail. He was not only visiting a minor branch store when his idea dawned—he was visiting it on a Saturday afternoon. This may serve to emphasize the basic lesson, that the highest executives can save no others until they have saved themselves. The man whose life is devoted to paperwork has lost the initiative. He is dealing with things that are brought to his notice, having ceased to notice anything for himself. He has been essentially defeated by his job.

To illustrate this point, let us compare the daily routine of two Managing Directors, whose names, purely imaginary, are Pending and Leederman. Pending arrives at the office to find his in-tray piled to the height of $18\frac{3}{4}''$. Of this stack $11\frac{1}{2}''$ comprise the information that Pending has demanded, and the remainder consists of files on which his decision is asked. Hardly has he looked at the first item before the day's mail is added. Of this additional $8''$, a fair proportion consists of circulars from the Board of

Trade. For paper of this kind every office has a suitable receptacle, but the rest of the mail needs answering. The process of dictation has scarcely begun when the first telephone call is received. With a staff conference at 11.30, lasting nearly an hour, and with continual interruptions of every kind, Pending fights back against the tide of paper. For a time it may seem that the flood is gaining on him. With a supreme effort, however, he masters it. The level begins to fall. With everything thrown into the battle, with blood, sweat and tears, Pending disposes of all the business on hand. By the time he leaves the office every letter has been answered, every problem solved and the in tray left empty. 'I have won again,' he reflects as he goes wearily to his car. He has earned his salary and doubts whether anyone else could have done as much. But what will happen if he goes sick? He can just cope if all goes well. But what if it doesn't? Some day it won't.

Mr Leederman has an outlook which is totally different. For him the flood of correspondence is merely an interruption. Were it to occupy the day, as happens with Pending, Leederman would think that his time had been wasted. This outlook is reflected in his routine. His mail is opened at 8.45 and the rule of the office is that fifty letters *must* be dealt with by 9.15. Leederman often replies in his own handwriting, usually at the foot of the document he has received. His answers are laconic: 'Sorry—can't be done,' 'O.K. I'll be there,' 'I quite agree,' and, occasionally, 'DRIVEL!' To other letters he dictates a brief reply. Brief it must be, for those not answered by 9.15 will have to be answered by someone else. That is the moment at which his dictation stops. At 9.20 there is a staff meeting which lasts no more than ten minutes and at which outstanding problems are dealt with verbally. The meeting over, Leederman grabs the telephone and attempts to make eight long-distance calls before 9.40. He has found by experience that the lines are more likely to be free then and that the same calls, made later in the morning, would take twice as long. At 10.0 he quits his desk and leaves the office, beginning a leisurely tour of the factory or setting off on a visit to a branch establishment. Instead of tearing round the factory so as to get back to the office, he tears through the office work in order to have time for the factory. He greets the elderly foreman, 'Hallo, Fred—how's it going?' 'Tell me, Bill, how's that new lad shaping on No. 5?' He feels pipes to see whether they are too hot. He notices a light left on in daylight. He sees a blocked gutter and tells someone to clear it. He asks after a man's wife, whom he knows to have been ill. And all the time he is noticing things and talking, his mind is revolving round a new idea. How would it be if they installed a gantry in No. 11 shed, making a new loading point at the back? Pondering this problem, he spots a boy he has never seen before. 'Who is the ginger-haired lad over there?' Later that day the awe-stricken youth will be telling his mother 'The Boss actually spoke to me, asked me which school I had been at—just like as if he was interested!' If there is any trouble in Leederman's factory—and there seldom is—he sees it coming from a mile off. If the place were to catch fire, he would be the first man on the spot; a fact which everyone seems to have realized.

It is just the same at the branch establishments. Leederman always tells them when he is coming. Why? Because, he says, the value of the visit lies half in the tidying-up

process which precedes it—the lick of paint on the previous day. He would have achieved something even if the
visit had to be cancelled at the last moment. But his visits
are never cancelled and never even hurried. He sees
everything, even the new tennis court. He has lunch in the
staff canteen, taking care to meet everybody beforehand
in the club-house. If there is a lack of leadership, a decline
in loyalty, that is the time when he detects it. His theory is
that the strained relationships are obvious from the way
people group themselves. When he sees the branch manager
at one end of the room, surrounded by a group of executives, while the rest are grouped at the other end of the
room, surrounding a senior departmental head, he senses
at once that there is something wrong. What precisely
is wrong he may not immediately guess but he rarely
leaves the place before he has found out. Should he stay
the night, as he often does, the head office staff know that
he will ring up at exactly 9.20 next morning. By then
his mail will have been opened and his deputy will have
framed fifteen or twenty questions, to each one of which
the answer can be 'Yes' or 'No'. After five or six minutes
Leederman will ring off and turn once more to the things
that matter. There are people who believe that he is a very
good manager indeed.

The essence of Leederman's philosophy is that the good
manager retains the initiative. He does not allow himself
to be penned into his office by a flood of routine business.
He anticipates the questions before they have been put on
paper. He foresees the difficulties before they have turned
themselves into memoranda. He has gone out to meet
the trouble before it has really begun. Towards thus
gaining the initiative a useful first step is to rid oneself of a

common misconception about what matters most. To illustrate this misconception, picture Mr Tangible (Sales Manager of Steeply, Rising, Ltd) calling on Mr Phonewright, Managing Director of the Longworthy-Faroff Group.

PHONEWRIGHT: 'Come in, Mr Tangible! Sit down. I'm glad to see you. Smoke? Do forgive me for one moment while I sign these letters . . . (*pause, scribbling*) . . . And I have to answer this message from the Works' Engineer—sorry! . . . (*pause, more scribbling. Telephone rings*). That you Henry? Oh, good! That's fine! I'll see your new plant when I get the chance—don't get much time though. What's that? Maybe you could put that in writing. Yes, I see that. But what about the overheads? No, it's not that simple, Henry. There's the accountants to satisfy and the Board to convince. Phone back later when you have the figures I asked for. O.K., Henry. That will be fine. G'bye. . . . Sorry about this, Mr Tangible. Where was I? Yes, I had this message to answer . . . (*pause, scribbling. Telephone rings*) . . . Bob! I was just going to ring you. Yes, yes, I heard about that. Too bad, too bad. Has she recovered? That's good. Look, Bob, I've thought again about what we were discussing yesterday. I think it can be managed, but whoever we put in charge will have to be good. Who? No, Bob, Joe couldn't do it. Besides, he will be on another assignment. Think it over! G'bye. . ., (*pause, scribbling. Telephone rings*) . . . That you, Peter? Golf next Sunday? Good idea. Shall I ask Roger? O.K. then. Who'll be the fourth man? . . . But, look, Peter, he's not quite in our class, is he? What's his handicap? . . . I suppose he must have improved, but still . . . certainly, I know that! . . .

Peter, I have another idea. Suppose we ask Neville? . . . etc., etc., etc. (*Tangible goes quietly out of the room and borrows a telephone at the Commissionaire's desk.*) . . . 'All right then, Peter—I'll see you Sunday. How's the family? Splendid! Where were you going on holiday this year? . . . But you went there last year! Well, that's true . . . Oh, we were thinking of going to Spain . . . No, Sheila never went before . . . O.K. then. See you on Sunday! . . . (*pause. Phonewright looks vaguely around. Wasn't there somebody waiting to see him? Odd! Oh well. He scribbles afresh. Telephone rings*). 'Who's that? Oh, Mr Tangible? Good to hear your voice! Yes, we were very interested indeed in the heavy equipment you have to offer. . . . Yes, yes. . . . Right then, we'll start with two of them, on trial. . . . Yes, it will be a large order if we are satisfied. . . . Fifty, at least, and maybe a hundred by the end of the year. What would the price be on fifty or more? . . . Come, you could give us a better discount than that! . . . Oh, I know . . . Well, send two of them and we'll see. G'bye.'

The misconception here is that everything should take priority over the man who is actually present. This would make sense if Phonewright were deliberately showing Tangible where he gets off. It would be a reasonable method of indicating that Steeply, Rising Ltd is an organization of no great repute or importance. But that is not Phonewright's motive. He is merely working on the assumption that a piece of paper is more important than a caller and a telephone more important than either. It is not that he regards Henry, Bob and Peter as top-ranking in themselves. He simply gives priority to a telephone as such, a fact which his colleagues have realized. It involves, as a habit, the risk of misjudging character and the certainty of losing business.

Where paper is concerned, public administration has had a bad effect on business. For while the civil servant's methods may be similar, his aims are different. For him, the file is an end in itself. Why? Because there is always the possibility of a public inquiry. At any stage of his career, questions may be asked as affecting his work. What action did he take in response to this? Was he the man responsible for recommending that? Whom did he consult before rejecting the other? So what the civil servant needs to protect himself is a file recording exactly what he has done. On receiving the application from A he laid it before his next superior B, having first obtained a legal opinion from C, which came to be embodied in Minute 43, dated March 27th. Advised by B, D then took action as follows' . . . The civil servant wants to show that he took the right decision, gave the right advice, asked the right questions and obtained the right facts before placing the right minute before the right authority. What actually *happens* is of little consequence. It is the file that has to be in order, not the people or things to which the file relates. There is a riot, we will suppose, at the prison, with two warders killed and five injured, the carpentry shop burnt and ten convicts at large. When the telegram arrives the official's concern is more with the file than the prison. What action would look best for the record? How best to ensure that the blame is not fixed on the official's department? What form of inquiry will produce the most soothing report? This attitude may be inevitable among civil servants but it is unhelpful in business. For there the distribution of blame does not lessen the fact that the large order has been cancelled, the client lost, the contract awarded to another firm and the goods not up to sample. In business the concern should not be with the file as such but with the people and the things. The Branch Manager may be sacked for showing too small a yield on the capital outlay, the correctness of his procedure being no excuse. The neatness of the file will console nobody, in fact, for the losses incurred.

What is to be done about this paper flood? It is no answer to prefer the telephone to the typewriter for while both consume time, the former does not even record what has been agreed. It is no answer to hold frequent conferences, with everyone flown there and back. Root cause of the paper torrent is the urge to over-centralize, an urge which exists in the nature of things. For centralization, up to a point, is inevitable. In so far as a chain store enjoys an advantage over a small family retail business, its greater efficiency must derive mainly from a centralized system of purchase and distribution. That there must be some control is manifest. The problem is to decide how far it should go and at what point it should be relaxed. Where should central policy give place to local initiative? No complete and final answer to this question is possible. If we are seeking criteria, however, by which to judge the point at which centralization should stop, one criterion might be the size of the head office staff in relation to the total numbers employed. Of the relevant facts this is at any rate one.

There is a strange and general reluctance to fix a normal ratio between administrative and other costs. Conceding, as we must, that businesses differ and that departures from the ideal are bound to occur, it would still seem possible to discover an acceptably economic ratio, departures from which could at least be explained. When challenged, some business men will mention, uncertainly, a tentative figure of 15 per cent; more as a maximum, perhaps, than as an ideal. British Universities spend between 10 per cent and 6 per cent on administration. There are allegedly fighting services in which administrative expenditure seems to dwarf all other types of expense. There is a distinction to be drawn, however, between the percentage spent on administration as a whole, and the proportion of that which goes to the head office. For the first and larger percentage is an indication of general efficiency (or incompetence), the second a very rough measure of the degree in which the organization is centralized. In one very competent firm the head office staff comprises 2.34 per cent of the total employed, the proportionate expense being somewhat higher. There may well be a number of efficient firms in which about 10 per cent goes on administration and half that on the central office. In general, the greater the central demand for statistics, returns and reports, the larger must be the staff needed if only for filing them. If they are to be digested and analysed, that means more staff and any consequent action (whether by way of praise or reproof) will mean more staff again. As collection, analysis, action and follow-up all represent successive degrees of control, the size and cost of the head office staff would seem to indicate, roughly, how much control there is. Where there is too much, it will probably cost too much. Were a perfect ratio to be established it would not be perfect in every case. There is no reason to suppose that what is perfect for a retail store chain would be perfect for (say) the National Coal Board. The fact remains, however, that a wide comparison of staff ratios would at least provide some food for thought. If the ideal solution were not apparent, we might at least remark some departures from the norm.

While a high proportion of the paper in circulation represents an over-centralized control, a rising proportion reflects nothing more than an urge to circulate. With modern duplicating methods it is as easy to provide fifty copies as ten. This being so, the human tendency is to order the larger number. Should extra copies be wanted, it is good to have them ready and relatively inexpensive to have them made. It is another human tendency, however, to distribute copies you have. It saves cupboard space for one thing. It also prevents people complaining afterwards that they were never told. So the distribution list is planted, one might say, in a fertile soil. It tends to lengthen and expand, blossom and ramify. Copies must go to all executives, all foremen, all supervisors and consultants. There must be copies for all specialists in economics, statistics, welfare, psychology, method, publicity, training and youth. There must be copies for the lawyer, the doctor, the accountant and dentist, the detective and scoutmaster, storeman and nurse. Copies must be placed on all notice-boards, in all recreation rooms, in every lavatory and on every door. All, but *all* must be informed. One result of this wide distribution is to be measured in the inches of paper on every desk. Another is that nobody reads what everyone gets. Nor would anyone who did have time for anything else.

The urge to circulate, which is prevalent in business, and endemic in government, reaches its worst excesses in the field of scientific learning. In research establishments, for example, the greatest efforts are concentrated on keeping the scientists in touch with each other's work and progress. Whole departments are devoted to this, producing a copious flood of printed and mimeographed memoranda. When a research department grows beyond a certain size we are told that the need for internal co-ordination overshadows the need for actual research. Perfect co-ordination is achieved only when there is nothing to co-ordinate. This internal problem might be regarded as serious; and so no doubt it is. Dwarfing it, however, is the problem posed by the scientific journal. For the tendency of learned periodicals to multiply has a bearing on the assumption that all periodicals should be read. Why, to begin with, should they multiply? Because each must fall, sooner or later, into the clutches of a professor (A) more fanatically jealous than the average. Under his editorship no article is accepted with which he does not agree and no book kindly reviewed other than those written by his own former pupils. The rival professor (B) whose articles have been most consistently excluded will then, and inevitably, start another journal; one edited at first on more liberal principles. B will accept articles from all who are not actual and known adherents of A. He eventually draws the line, however, at contributions from C, whose works are confused, long, and original only in their grammar and punctuation. But C realizes by now where his remedy lies. He becomes the founder of a new and less hidebound periodical; one more open at first to new and confused ideas. There is a difficulty, in the end, however, over the articles submitted by D, who cannot even spell. But D is not to be denied access to the misprinted page. He hesitates, to be sure, before adding one more journal to the library shelves; but not for long. His

duty is clear and he does not shirk it. And so the process
continues until there are eighty journals or more in den-
tistry alone. As for the whole field of learning, the figures
are staggering, and not the least so in their rate of increase.
A University library may take up to 33,000 periodicals.
Each learned journal will have a council, an editor, sub-
editors and staff. Each must involve a great deal of work.
And the final result, as seems sufficiently well known, is
that the few scientists who matter exchange their ideas in
private correspondence. It has also been argued that the
multiplication of journals is in inverse proportion to the
progress made. With less time wasted on editing and reading there would be more time, possibly, in which to work
and think.

If scientific journals tend to multiply, trade and technical
publications certainly become no fewer. On to the desk
of the senior executive there pours a torrent of paper
and he will be judged at first on his ability to deal with it.
This can be initialled as seen. This other must be referred
to a higher level. Here is one that must be answered and
here another that can be ignored. Refer this back as incomplete and the next as incorrect, say 'Yes' to this and
'No' to that, expedite one and lose the other. Have that
filed and this destroyed, mark these as urgent and let those
wait. Retype this as corrected and make a draft reply to
that. Check by telephone whether the reply means what
it says and confirm verbally that you say what you mean.
Total the figures again and compare them with the estimate. Verify the spelling of Vaaderschnelling's name and
decipher, if possible, his Works Manager's signature. Ask
White to call tomorrow and tell Black to chase himself.
Thank Brown for his help and tell Green to pull himself

together. Give Sylvia some typing to do as she looks idle
and send Jean home because she looks ill. Don't let the
paper mount high in the in-tray. Don't let the pending
get heaped on the floor. Deal with the paper, answer and
file it, read it and sign it and send for some more.

SECUNDITY

Beyond all reasonable expectation, you now find the summit within reach. You stand second in the hierarchy and may soon (who knows?) be first. You will have played second fiddle before but not at this rarefied altitude. The time has come for that last great effort on which your future must depend. How to be the perfect Number Two? Here is a question demanding the most careful analysis. We are faced at the outset, however, with a problem of nomenclature. By what official title is your secundity to be defined? Terms of status are apt to prove misleading and fluid. Behind their imprecisions there loom, however, the hard facts of life. In nearly every big organization there is a Number One. There is also, and almost as inevitably, a Number Two.

There they are and have always been, and there presumably they will always be. In primitive societies the family group is headed by the father or the grandfather, 'the old man' (as a ship's Master is still called) to whom his eldest son stands as Number Two, deputy, and presumed successor. All human authority has this paternal origin, being based on wonder, affection and fear; wonder felt by a child when witnessing his father's skill, affection for a protector who is interested in securing the child's survival, and fear of the punishment which the father, as teacher, is bound to inflict. The office of Number Two, or eldest (or, alternatively, ablest) son has thus a respectable antiquity.

But does *every* organization have an acknowledged Number Two? No, there is a significant exception. In a political despotism or dictatorship there is no real deputy and no named successor. For the whole strength of the régime rests on the assumption that the current ruler is impossible to replace. After all, an effective deputy makes the ruler less indispensable. A known successor makes him less secure. It is part of the technique, therefore, of dictatorship to leave the second throne unfilled. Instead of Number Two there are several people in competition, the position of each weakened by the jealousy of the rest. Nor is dictatorship unknown in commerce and industry. There have been Corporations ruled in much the same way and usually with the same result; namely, that the organization lasts no longer than the man. The normal preference of mankind is for institutions of greater stability, for types of government which can survive a single bullet, for industrial empires which can survive a single heart attack. So that industrial dictatorships are more the exception than the rule.

Another exception to the normal is to be found where the Number Two is really the Number One. The whisper goes round that Mr Lurking is the man to see if you want results—not Mr Roger de Coverley, Managing Director though he may be. This sort of situation is not uncommon. There are men like Mr Lurking who hunger for power but not for office and they sometimes contrive to join forces with someone like de Coverley, who longs for office but not for power. It was thus at one time the German Army custom to select a Chief of Staff with meticulous care, appointing his Commander-in-Chief as a careless afterthought. There are examples, moreover, of such an inverted partnership proving successful, as it might often

prove in a society merely of men. Among a celibate priest-hood, as with a Cardinal and his confessor, this arrangement may often work well. But where one man is married there is an element of instability in the relationship; and where both are married there are two. The married chief who is dominated by his Number Two is also likely to be dominated by his wife; and she, resenting a rival's influence, will urge her husband to assert himself. Number Two's wife may be more submissive to Number Two but her grievance will lie in the almost insufferable airs of superiority assumed by the wife of Number One. The influence of the Bishop's lady in Trollope's novel was greater than that of the Bishop's chaplain, not merely be-cause she was more formidable but because she was more constantly at the Bishop's side. So it is in real life. And even were both men bachelors, who can guarantee that they will so remain? Where a single red-haired and pert-nosed secretary can bring about an internal revolution, the situation lacks stability. The pyramid stands better with its apex at the top.

Taking, then, the normal and preferable situation where Number One is actually as well as theoretically in charge, we must now consider the position of Number Two. Our temptation at the outset is to conclude that all Numbers Two are alike. It is so easy to picture the ideal Number Two—old Tom, old Dick, or old Harry, so *reliable*, so quietly efficient, always there when wanted, so tactfully absent when not required, so kind to the office staff and such a delightful uncle to Number One's children. But such incidental functions as these must not be allowed to cloud our vision. Numbers Two are *not* all the same. Some are self-effacing and obscure, others are mysterious and secretive. There is the Number Two who is genial but evasive and the opposite type who is negative and dumb. Some are effusively co-operative but foiled, it would seem, by the opposition of the Board. Others are obstructive and surly until outflanked by an appeal to higher authority. Numbers Two might seem, in fact, to offer an infinite variety in temperament and outlook. They actually fall, however, into two basic categories; those (A) who are content to be Number Two and those (B) who want to become Number One. It might not be easy to draw a firm line between the one category and the other—for some individuals are to be found in a state of transition—but the categories exist and the majority of Numbers Two can be placed in one or the other.

The inevitable and eternal Numbers Two, who lack, and perhaps have always lacked, any higher ambition, are easily distinguishable. They reveal a slight wandering of interest, a preoccupation with things not strictly within the organization. They talk of Ratepayers' Associations, Boards, local politics, Golf Clubs and the Chamber of Commerce. Their homes reveal an assumption that they will always be there—as in the cultivation of asparagus and the concreting of the drive. They are as active as ever, mind you—never more so—and never (well, hardly ever) late at the office. But they have passed the age of ambition and have begun to take a pride, rather, in the progress of their children; in their son's success at Oxford or their married daughter's firstborn. There is a settled, comfortable look about the predestined Number Two. He is to be identified more by that than by anything he says. From force of habit he may even go on talking of promotion but his words are belied by his appearance.

There is an art in being the contented Number Two, whether as one predestined from the start or as one whose role has been thrust upon him. It is the art, essentially, of identifying oneself with a hero. At the cinema or before the television screen the normal person will readily identify himself with the hero of the moment. He does not visualize the Western Set at the Studio and the director ordering a tenth retake of the first sequence. He does not wonder why people should always fall when hit and nevertheless rise unhurt. He just clenches his fists or allows his hand to hover over an imaginary holster, seeing the hero's prowess as his own. The ideal Number Two makes Number One his hero and assumes for himself a share of the drama. It is 'we' who take the decision and 'we' who quell the absurd proposals put forward at the Board Meeting. 'Number One knows all that goes on,' says Number Two. 'You can't fool *him*. He knows all the answers.' But the tone of his admiration cannot hide from us the fact that Number Two has projected himself into the part. Number One's achievement has become partly his. And Numbers Two (A) although they may differ at the outset, tend to become alike as time goes on. It is thus the duty of a Chief of Staff to write in the style of his Commander-in-Chief, so choosing his words that the despatch hardly needs alteration. The ideal Number Two speaks with the voice of his chief and has no separate views of his own.

Come now to category B, the probably larger group of Numbers Two whose ambition is to be Number One. These executives can be divided into three groups, (I), (II) and (III). Those in Group I were all appointed *since* Number One. Chosen by Number One himself from among the departmental heads, this type of deputy seems relatively young and optimistic, never (he says) having expected such promotion and never having held such high office before. 'Gosh!' he will exclaim. 'But it's splendid to work under a man like Alan Topleigh! I learn something new every day. He's a wonderful chap—and he does know his stuff! I know when I'm lucky.' Bubbling over with devotion, especially when within earshot of Mrs Topleigh, Bob Upton is obviously a Coming Man. He can't think why the chief should have picked on *him*, with so many good men to choose from, but there it is. Alan shall never regret his choice, not if Bob can help it. When Alan is away at a Conference, Bob shines as deputy. 'No,' he says, 'I don't think that is the decision that Alan would have made.' 'Yes,' he admits, 'that's pretty much in line with our policy.' 'As for that last item,' he concludes, 'I feel that had better wait until Alan gets back.' And when Alan Topleigh talks about retirement, it is Bob who leads the deputation that implores him to stay on. 'Maybe you need a holiday, sir, but we all want you back here at your desk. We still need you and we can't believe you're ready to retire.' Everyone agrees that Bob Upton is a first-rate fellow and that his star is in the ascendant.

In Group II are the Numbers Two who were appointed *before* Number One assumed his present post. Each was the choice of Number One's predecessor. Mark Waydown is a good example of a Number Two (B.II). He is the very best type of executive, efficient, co-operative and popular. Rumour has it that the Board took a chance on the present Number One, Mr Picton Young, and would never have done so had they not been able to rely on Waydown— the ideal man to help a chief whose experience (at that time) was hardly sufficient. And no one can deny that

Mark ('Daddy' to the juniors) has done a splendid job. He is not really so much older than Number One but he often seems elderly by comparison—and just a little inclined to fuss. But the organization would be nowhere, simply *nowhere* without him. If anyone knows the business, it is he. He knows everyone by name and is always ready with advice or help. It is he who remembers that a scheme like the one under discussion was tried before in 1937. If there is a complex job to do, Mark is the man to tackle it. He takes a simple pride in the way he is trusted by the Board. No one has never questioned his loyalty to Number One, even though some believe him to be the abler man of the two. 'Leave it to Mark,' says Number One, and the job, whatever it is, will be finished in time. If the firm's output can be said to depend on any one individual, Mark would be that man; or so most people think. He is more than valuable, he is *essential*.

In the same category and group as Mark Waydown but in a different industry is Carveth Carping, unquestionably one of the ablest executives in the Bellectronics business. Of Carping's ability there can be no doubt at all. He would have been Managing Director if Victor Peake had not happened to be available. A little older than Mark Waydown and looking older than he is, Carveth has never been more than civil to Victor. Eight years his junior, the Managing Director makes a show of friendly informality but it deceives nobody. As for Carveth, he overflows with unspoken criticism. Asked about the Company's policy, he outlines the current plan for development, shrugs his shoulders and adds, after a slight pause, 'Whether this scheme is the best we can do . . . well, time will show. Some of us have sometimes—oh, well, it doesn't matter now. You know Peake, of course? A remarkable man! I don't know how he does it—I really don't!' He is often heard to say, 'I don't know how he does it!' and there is just enough ambiguity about this to create despondency. Without uttering a word which could be called disloyal, Carveth throws doubts on each decision the chief takes. 'If we didn't *trust* Peake as we do, we might *almost* think he had misjudged the market trend, but I suppose he must know what he's doing. He has a sort of intuition, and that's more valuable, I dare say, than mere experience. We shall see . . .' Carveth is a master of pregnant silence—he could have taken his degree in it—and his raised eyebrows convey more distrust than words could express. From all Carveth omits to say, it is obvious that Peake's failure is complete.

Last of all, there is Group III, comprising former Numbers One, brought into the organization as the result of a merger. There is Brian Boughtover, for example, who became Number Two of the Giantsquid Group when his own Company (Frankleigh, Tottering & Co.) was absorbed in 1960. Relations between the Managing Director and Brian are too polite to be convincing. 'Let's ask Brian's opinion before we go any farther,' says Cecil Summit. 'Oh, no, Cecil,' says Brian, 'your judgement is best—I would rather be guided by you.' 'Thank you, Brian, but you have more experience in this particular field.' 'I wouldn't say that, Cecil—I believe you know more than any of us.' 'You are too modest, Brian,' etc., etc. So the discussion goes on, Cecil devoutly wishing that Brian were not there, and Brian wishing as fervently that he were somewhere else. The Number One reduced in rank presents a frequent problem in the world of business and one to which there is usually only one solution: Brian's retirement or transfer.

If we analyse and compare the present position of these four representative Numbers Two, we realize at once that Bob Upton is the only one certain of promotion. In the ordinary way, we should expect him to leave shortly in order to accept the Managing Directorship of a smaller concern in the same line of business. This appointment will be on Alan Topleigh's recommendation, his private letter emphasizing that Bob is the best man he has ever trained. Three years later, Topleigh will retire and Bob will be his obvious successor. No such good fortune awaits Mark Waydown, who is indispensable (as Number Two). Picton Young will never release him. Should Mark put in for the top post elsewhere, at his wife's insistence, Picton's letter of recommendation will lay stress on his loyalty and competence while subtly throwing doubt on his fitness to be Number One. 'As actual head of an organization, Mr Waydown is untried, but of this I am certain, that he will always do his utmost.' With this kind of support, Mark is sure of second place on any short list, and second he will remain unless the man chosen should actually burst a blood vessel and drop dead on being offered the post. The question often asked is whether Mark really wants more responsibility than he has. Who can tell? Certainly not Mark himself, in whom disappointment and relief are nicely balanced. The truth is, maybe, that he was more ambitious to begin with and is less ambitious now. But rejecting an applicant is very much a matter of habit. Whoever has been rejected once will usually be rejected again. And whoever has been passed over once, the appointment going to a younger man, will *certainly* be passed over again. To appoint him on a later occasion would be tantamount to admitting that the earlier rejection was a mistake; which is absurd. So Mark's chances of promotion are in inverse proportion to his present usefulness. His chances are dwindling and will presently vanish.

But Mark's chances, slight as they are, look hopeful when compared with those of Carveth Carping. The position of these two men is basically the same (B.II), each having seen a younger man preferred. It is their reaction that has been different. To the man passed over, two obvious courses are open. He can show by his loyal co-operation that there is no vice in him. Or else he can show, by proof of superior intelligence, that the decision against him was unquestionably wrong. Either course is fatal but the latter more immediately so. For the mutual dislike between Peake and Carping must produce a state of deadlock. Carping would go, as Number One, to a smaller Company, but Peake will never support his claim. In theory, Peake should be anxious to get rid of him and so indeed he is. But this anxiety is seldom so strongly felt as to produce a glowing testimonial. Carping's actual promotion is too high a price to pay for his removal. The mutual loathing felt for each other by Peake and Carping is the force, in fact, which keeps them together. And were Peake to find the situation intolerable he would almost certainly frustrate himself in a different way. For his letters of support would become too effusive as well as too numerous. Beyond a certain point enthusiasm arouses suspicion.

'If this chap is really such a ball of fire why is Peake so keen to get rid of him?'

'Maybe he makes Peake feel small.'

'In that case we can't give much weight to Peake's recommendation. Let's take another look at Ratrace again, the Number Two at Savage, Striving, Ltd.' So Carping is not even placed. And the more consistently he is proved right, the farther down the list does his name appear. Who wants a man who is always saying, 'I told you so'? In the ordinary course of events Carping is doomed to frustration. Had he been made Number One in the first place he would have been as good as Peake or better. But disappointment has spoilt his character as well as his prospects. He is no longer in the hunt.

And what of Brian Boughtover? His prospects are relatively good. There is a certain fraternity among Numbers One, a feeling of club membership. Once in, you are always in, at least for some purposes; and once out, you stand a fair chance of re-admission. If Brian is not too near the age of retirement he will have Summit's help towards a new position as Number One. It will not do to have former Numbers One on the labour market. It lowers the status of the others, serving as a reminder of what can befall any one of them. There is an unspoken rule that the man displaced should, if possible, be hauled back on to the raft. What is least desirable is to have Brian still there as Number Two.

From this study of Numbers Two (A) who are content as they are, and Numbers Two (B) who long for promotion, it will be apparent that the role to avoid is that of a Number Two (B) to whom promotion is denied. So much is clear enough: but what if this is the role that has been thrust upon you? It can happen to any of us. So let the reader suppose, for a minute, that it has happened to him. You have been rejected for the top post, let us imagine, and the man chosen is six years your junior. You might your-self be content, in time, to remain Number Two, but your wife is NOT content to be the Number Two Wife. She has begun to give you the pitying glance which is reserved for the world's predestined Numbers Two. Your daughter has been heard to refer to you as 'Poor old pop.' The situation is serious, not to say critical, and it is a case of Now or Never. What are you to do?

The starting-point for your pondering is this question: 'Were they right to pass you over?' So far, in discussing the position of Mark Waydown, Carveth Carping, Bob Upton and Brian Boughtover, we have assumed that all these Numbers Two are capable, or were once capable, of being Number One. There are many Numbers Two of whom this can fairly be said. But there are others, equally am-bitious and undoubtedly able, who would fail if promoted. Nor shall we understand the essential character of a Number Two unless we can analyse his short-comings. What distinguishes the Natural Number One from the inevitable but frustrated Number Two? You are too modest to press your own claims so we shall ask your wife whether the Board was right to reject you. Suppose that her reply is on these lines:

'Right? Are you crazy? Everyone knows that Tony is the better man. He has been the brains of the business for years. After all, he ought to understand the trade, having joined the staff in 1946, just when he came out of the Navy. How he worked in those early days, when we were first married! He used to work all night so as to have the answer ready when the boss wanted some information. Tony is a worker all right. And then, everyone likes him. Yes, *everyone*. There is never a grumble if Tony says that people must stay on at the office. They know that it must be necessary, and they know that he'll be the last to leave. Though I say it myself, Tony is the very best man they could have chosen. And what do they do? They find this Upward fellow and his cheap-looking wife. It's the craziest thing they ever did.'

Let us suppose that all she says is true. You are all she thinks and more. But we still have no proof that you are Number One material. *Are you?* It is your own answer to this question that is important. You must believe in yourself before others can believe in you. Your own verdict comes first and it may be final. Newspapers sometimes carry self-marking questionnaires in which people are invited to assess their own qualities, often on the basis of twenty questions or more. For you, for the man who has already come so far towards success, for a perfectly competent Number Two, there are only three questions, and they are as follows:

QUESTION ONE: *When you have a cold or high temperature, on what day of the week does it begin?* Think back carefully. Maybe you will answer, 'Well it might begin any day, I suppose. Can't say I've really noticed.' If that is your answer, Number Two is your right level. For the predestined Number One will answer without hesitation: 'All my ailments begin on Friday afternoon and I always recover by Monday morning.' The point is that a Number Two destined to be Number One must never go sick, or not at least until years after his promotion. Everyone else can have influenza if they like and can have it during the same week, as they often do, but that makes it all the more vital that *you* should be there. And at your desk you will be found, let the epidemic be what it may. But can the onset of an illness be thus controlled by the patient? It certainly can. You make no deliberate effort but in the natural boss (if you are one) the ailment is subconsciously held in check. There is some internal mechanism which keeps the germs on the leash from Monday to Friday. 'You can't be ill now,' it whispers, 'there's the staff meeting this afternoon.' 'There's the lunch for Lord Dimwit,' it hisses. 'You can't begin sneezing yet.' This built-in mechanism works perfectly until Friday midday. Although no longer on top form, you deal with all the urgent business and begin signing the outgoing mail at about 3.30. It is then that your secretary observes for the first time that you are not looking well. As she comments on this, using that tone of motherly solicitude which she was made to rehearse at the Secretarial College, you sneeze. 'Oh, dear, Mr Toplevel, I do believe you have a touch of flu!' You realize that she is (as always) right, and the internal mechanism suddenly lets go, muttering, 'All right! Give it the works!' You can be as sick as you like—until Sunday midnight. Away you stagger, hardly able to stand upright. You retire to bed with a hot whisky and lemon. Your temperature reaches 102° that night and you wonder whether you have a fifty-fifty chance of survival. None can be so desperately ill as those whose general health is excellent. By Saturday midday you send for your solicitor (who can't be found, having gone fishing), saying that you must alter your will—a matter of some small bequest to a medical research foundation. By Saturday night you are on the point of death. On Sunday morning you are recovering. During the afternoon you are convalescent. And by Monday morning you are back at your desk and perfectly well. The existence or absence of this internal mechanism is a simple question of fact. If you don't have it, you are not of the stuff of which Numbers One are made. You have it? Yes? Then go on to the next question.

QUESTION TWO: *Are you prepared to do whatever the other fellows can't or won't?* In theory, everyone on the pay-roll is there to do what he or she is told. In practice, however, they do as they like. One has a taste for public relations and another likes to file documents where they can never again be found. One loves to draw up organization charts and another goes round switching off the lights. But there is one man who cannot do what he likes and that is Number One. For on him devolves, in addition to his normal work, the job that is left over; and no one can guess what that is going to be. It may be working out the vacation roster or it may be choosing the paint. It might be checking the gas consumption and then again it might be testing the fire drill. It could be having the windows cleaned or it could be mending the fuse. But whatever it may chance to be, there is nobody left to do it—except Number One. It is what no one else will do that falls, in the end, to him. Are you prepared for this and cheerfully confident? You are? Then go on to the last question—which is not so easy.

QUESTION THREE: *Are you prepared to sack Joe Wittering?* You know him, of course. Every organization has or has had a Joe Wittering. He is quite honest and very generally liked and is one of the most well-meaning fellows alive. He bumbles around harmlessly with unanswered letters in his pocket, breakfast smears on his tie, cigarette ash on his trousers and a vacant smile on his face. Joe is known to everybody as a kindly old muddler with a popular wife and five children at school. There might be a case for retaining Joe but we'll suppose that there isn't. In another organization he might have been useful, even invaluable, as the man who is always wrong (*see Chapter 7*). But times are hard, competition is keen, money is scarce and we can't afford to make any more mistakes. Joe has to be fired. As Number One, it is your job and no one else's to send for Joe and say: 'You are not good enough for this Company and I am abolishing your post as from October 1st. You have until then to find yourself another job. Short of perjury, I shall do what I can for you.' His face will go white and his hands will tremble. He will stammer something about his past work, about his wife and kids, to which you will reply: 'I'm sorry, Joe, but my decision is final.' You are ready to do that? But this is not the whole of the test. For, having looked Joe Wittering in the eyes and said, 'You're sacked,' you have to go home and sleep soundly, not having given the matter another thought.

To be a good Number Two (which you are) you need knowledge, skill, ability and tact. All these you need as Number One but with something else, that touch of ruthlessness which distinguishes the man at the top. It may be a General's duty to order the blowing of a bridge, knowing that some of his own troops are still on the other side. It may fall to a ship's Commander to close the watertight bulkhead, with stokers trapped beyond. Nor is this sort of decision taken with cinematic emotion. It is done calmly and coldly, leaving only that permanently changed expression of the mouth and the eyes. Do you pass that final test in its lesser peacetime form? It is not merely a question, remember, of sacking Joe Wittering. You must

sleep soundly afterwards. There must be no wondering
'Did I do the right thing?', no guesses as to what the
Witterings will do, but an instant switching to the next
problem; which may indeed be the sacking of somebody
else.

We shall suppose now that you have given the right
answer to each of the three vital questions. All your ailments happen between Friday afternoon and Monday
morning. You are able and ready to do whatever job is
left over. And you are prepared to sack Joe Wittering.
With all your experience and ability and with the three
additional qualities that mark you out for leadership, you
have nevertheless been turned down. With a barely cred-
ible want of common sense, the Board have appointed
a younger man as chief, leaving you as Number Two.
Human failings being what they are, this sad fate could
befall anyone; and so, after years of successful work, it has
happened to you. The new Number One has arrived and
you have bid him welcome on behalf of the salaried staff.
You have added your own warm congratulations, noting
inwardly that his hair is thinning and that his suit is badly
tailored. Your wife considers that Number One's wife is
older than she pretends to be and that her taste in dress is
almost (well, let's face it) *dowdy*. The ceremonies are over
and now the question is—what are you to do next?

Until very recently there would have been no answer to
this question. The only hope for Number Two, we should
have had to admit, lies in the possibility of Number One
having a long and serious illness, leaving Number Two
well established by the time Number One actually resigns
or dies. But this sort of illness is, in fact, extremely unlikely.

In the words of the proverb, a watched pot never boils. The person who is to benefit from an annuity will live for ever. It is no good waiting for Number One to fall sick. The better policy is to manœuvre him out of the way. It was once believed that people could be forced to retire by a combination of form-filling and air-travel. Sound as it was in its day the method is no longer effective. Nor will this surprise anyone who has ever used insecticide. In the first years, as we know, an insecticide will produce some results; not killing the mosquitoes, perhaps, but definitely giving them the sense of being unwanted. In the second year their feelings are unhurt—they are used to it. In the third year they like it. And in the fourth year they quite possibly cannot live without it. So it is with our high executives. They have come to look upon aircraft with a tolerance bordering on affection. So the need arises for some other means of discouraging those senior to us. It is just such a secret that is now to be revealed for the first time.

This most Up-to-Date form of Number-One-Removal involves the application of Management Science. If you, as Number Two, are unfamiliar with Management Science, your first move should be to hire a Ph.D. from, say, Manchester. Experts in this field are numerous and cheap, so that there should be no difficulty in recruiting a Management Scientist from a Business School. Suppose that the one chosen is Dr Hellkite, whose wife is herself a known specialist in Behaviour. You persuade Number One to allow the Head Office to be made the subject of a technical investigation. The whole programme will be at the expense (you will explain) of the Hecate Institute, which has provided three research assistants. And now the staff meeting is to receive the first Interim Report.

DUNCAN: Item 3. Report from Dr Hellkite, copies of which have been circulated, Any comments?

MACBETH: I suggest, sir, that we invite Dr Hellkite to explain his project. Here he is. . . .

DUNCAN: Very well, Number Two. Dr Hellkite, the floor is yours.

HELLKITE: My object, gentlemen, is to present our Interim Report in the simplest form. The facts already revealed call for immediate action. To wait for the final report would be to let the situation deteriorate. Briefly, then, I have made a preliminary study of this organization, using Batworthy's non-linear extension of the optimal range. . . .

MACBETH: With internal validity checks, I hope?

HELLKITE: Certainly. You will find a note on diagnostic procedures at Appendix K. Applying a strategy of random variables and using the Stochastic Model; applying, more-over, our experience of operations research and decision theory, we could not escape the meaningful conclusion which we have tabulated on pages 34 to 37.

DUNCAN: Very interesting, but I really don't see . . .

MACBETH: Forgive my interrupting, sir, but I think I can explain the passage which you find obscure. I was puzzled myself and asked Dr Hellkite why he rejected the simpler strategy of Filkenstein's Theorum. But he soon convinced me that quadratic programming would not, in this case, have been helpful. I think you will find the report in other respects both lucid and cogent.

Pause now and reflect, for the staff meeting has reached what is known in the bullfighting arena as the Moment of Truth. For Number One it is a question of Now or Never. To regain control of the situation he must at this point drop his copy of the Interim Report into the wastepaper basket and address Dr Hellkite in some such words as these:

DUNCAN: All this sounds to me like froth and gas. I haven't the least idea what you are talking about and have no reason to think that it matters. If you have any constructive comments to make on our organization, make them in plain language, stating what you think should be done. But don't talk to me as you might to a digital computer. I don't like it, don't grasp it and won't have it.

By this brusque reaction, which will reduce Dr Hellkite to twittering ineptitude, Number One can defeat the whole plot. In a moment all those present will be admitting in chorus that the Interim Report is so much meaningless drivel. The founder of the Company, old Tom Tuffenuff, would have done exactly that. But today's executives are seldom men of his calibre. It takes some courage to profess a scornful ignorance among a whole group of executives, each professing to follow the whole argument. In nine cases out of ten, Number One will fail the test. He will nod his head in feigned comprehension. And once the moment has passed, he will never regain control of the meeting, which will continue on these lines:

DUNCAN: Thank you, Mac. The Report might have been worded more clearly, but I think we all understand the Doctor's point. (*He looks round.*)

ALL: (*Quickly*) Yes, yes. Perfectly clear.

MACBETH: Well, I seem to be the dunce here, but I'm still puzzled by the last half of page 41. Why should dynamic programming involve the theory of games?

HELLKITE: I'm glad you asked that. My symbol manipulation language is not as coherent as it should be. The page summarizes my heuristic line-balancing procedure, which leads to the non-basic optimum solution on the next page.

MACBETH: But that solution is inconsistent, surely, with the combination analysis and topology on page 17—look, you say here that

$$\Pi = \frac{1}{mm} - (p + h^2)$$

What about the calculus of probabilities?

HELLKITE: It doesn't apply to a multiperson interaction. It *would* have applied, I freely admit, had I been using a different methodology. But the conclusions would have been much the same.

MACBETH: Oh, I'm not questioning that. The Zoning-Constraint would not have been affected.

HELLKITE: Exactly! It is a question of cybernetics and a use of the minimax principle. We are basically in agreement, I think.

MACBETH: That is so. But your exhaustive algorithms leave me with a regret function which defies analysis.

HELLKITE: (*Laughing heartily*) Good, good!

ALL: (*Smiling nervously*) He, he, he. . . .

MACBETH: Well, sir. We have, as I see it, to apply this Report to the Activation of Motives in our organization. I suggest, however, that we defer action until Part II of the final report is before us, which will be in about three weeks' time. The matter can wait until then, I imagine, but not much longer—isn't that right?

HELLKITE: We need a firm decision before the end of the month.

MACBETH: Right. And we shall need to discuss Part II at some length before we outline our programme.

DUNCAN: (*Apprehensively*) At some length?

MACBETH: Well, we need to know what we are doing.

DUNCAN: (*Crushed*) I suppose so. . . .

MACBETH: And I feel we should thank Dr Hellkite for all his help.

ALL: Yes, yes. Very valuable indeed.

HELLKITE: I could never have produced this Interim Report without the help of the three research assistants provided for me by the Hecate Institute. Miss Weard and her two sisters have done a fine job. Might I convey to them the Company's thanks?

DUNCAN: I suppose so.

HELLKITE: They will greatly appreciate it.

DUNCAN: And now, Dr Hellkite, you will be wanting to get back to your investigations. Thank you, Doctor. . . .

Now—Item 4. The estimate for repairing the power-house roof. Mr Macduff?

Number One will bluster over Item 4 but he has nevertheless lost ground. By next week he will have to face another discussion with Dr Hellkite and still without the least idea of what is to be discussed. Then will come the final report. In this Dr Hellkite will include his masterpiece, the Model to illustrate the Head Office Social System. As this represents the last deadly stroke, it is worth reproducing in full. Here it is:

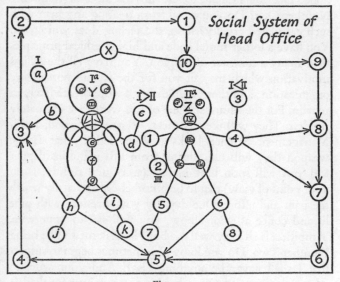

Figure 1

At the sight of this diagram, Number One will utter a hollow groan. 'Oh, *no*!' he will whisper, 'not *that*!' But *that*

is nevertheless what he has to face. All he can do is to retire
to bed with a migraine, leaving Number Two to carry out
the planned reorganization. Whenever Number One shows
signs of recovery, a mere flourish of the diagram (Figure 1),
a mere distant echo of Dr Hellkite's voice, will be enough
to bring on a relapse. The time for Number One's retirement is near and there can be no doubt as to who his
successor must be. Nor is there any doubt as to what you
do with Dr Hellkite as soon as the farewells have been said.
'Out!' you will say briefly, proving once more that the
hired assassin becomes unwelcome after the deed has been
done. Do you hesitate to use this method of removing
Number One? Do you recoil from treating any man with
such calculated cruelty? If so, the feeling does you credit.
You have a loftier moral code and higher ethical principles
than many a minister of religion. You have all the selfless
motivation which may fit you for the second post in any
organization; and there, as Number Two, you are likely to
remain. For the Numbers One of this world are ultimately
ruthless. They will use any means to gain their end, and if
Management Science looks usefully lethal, that is the
weapon they will use. Shrink from this nebulous dagger
and you will soon be thinking (and quite rightly, from
your point of view) that to be Number One is hardly worth
the pain and effort. One day, by your fireside, with pipe
lit and coffee at your elbow, you will say to your wife,
'Ambition is all very well . . . but I have come to like being
Number Two. Do you know, I sometimes begin to suspect
that I shall never be anything else?' And your wife, to
whom the same suspicion has been a certainty for the last
six years, will calmly and smilingly agree.

THE 'PARKINSEY REPORT

An industrial empire such as you aspire to rule is not a mechanical structure in which steel girders rest on concrete blocks. It is rather the result of a biological process in which seed and mating, growth and fertility play the dominant role. The world of business is an avenue in which parasites cling to the trees; a garden where weeds spring up among the flowers; an orchard in which bees carry the pollen of managerial science from one plant to another; a wood in which the branches of economic theory are strictly for the birds. In this wonderland of nature the facts of life are not to be ignored. One such fact is sex and we should be wrong to pretend otherwise. Victorian authors who dealt with the business world were reticent about the sexual aspect although all too prone to Smiles of furtive innuendo. Today we have learnt to discuss these matters frankly and openly, giving our children illustrated pamphlets about the flowers and the bees and telling each other (perhaps too often) that the mysteries of nature are really very beautiful. We can no longer disguise the fact that the Limited Liability Company has Sex.

Like any flower or shrub the industrial plant is either male or female. There are not, to be sure, the external sex differences observable in the animal world. Sex determination in business is a matter therefore for the expert. Your success in life may depend, however, on your becoming such an expert. Before joining the Board of a Company you must discover its sex. Nor is this as difficult as some

authors have chosen to pretend. After all, sex characteristics in a Company are broadly similar to those found
in a human being. Do not so oversimplify the problem,
however, as to identify the corporate sexes as Sale and
Resale. While there may be a male tendency in wholesale
business and a female bias in the retail, it would be quite
wrong to think that this is invariable. Such a crude analysis
would leave the sex undetermined in many an enterprise
while causing misunderstanding and subsequent embar-
rassment as a result of mistaking the sex of others. No
mistakes need be made by the observer who knows what
the sex characteristics are.

A male industrial organization is to be identified, first
of all, by its rough exterior. It may be fairly tidy but it has
made no effort to look attractive. The layout is more
practical than pleasing, the machinery unconcealed and
the paintwork conservative and drab. Combined with this
rugged appearance is an assertiveness in advertising, a
rather crude claim to offer what is at once the cheapest and
the best. The organization is extravert, outgoing and in-
quisitive, its representatives more likely to visit another
organization than wait to be visited by others. With this
type of Company's boastful manner goes a carelessness
over details, a failure to check the outgoing mail, a neglect
to clean the windows, an omission to test the fire appliance.
Added to all this is the male extravagance. Faced with a
decline in gross turnover, the male urge is not so much to
economize as to seek some other source of income. It has
been suggested that the male organization is polygamous,
showing a tendency to form temporary attachments or
engage at least in casual flirtations. This theory cannot be
accepted without certain reservations but that it has some

basis is undeniable. While many or perhaps most male organizations are loyal to their chief business associate, others have a roving tendency and all (it may be) a roving eye. Last of all, the male organization is apt to treat its male offspring with some severity, telling them to fight their own battles and punishing any whose gambling losses seem excessive.

The female organization shows all the opposite characteristics. Its factory buildings are prettily sited and smartly kept with pastel shades in the paintwork and flower beds near the gate. But with the attractive layout there goes a certain modesty. Some parts of the production process are usually concealed and there may be a certain reticence shown in other ways—as affecting past associations, for example, and even the age of the plant. In the female organization there can be too much fuss over details, an insistence on exact procedure and an over-emphasis on the appearance (as opposed to the reality) of competence. In general policy the female trend is towards economy and financial caution. Faced with a recession, the female organization hastens to curtail expenditure and reduce the dividend. In general negotiations this type of Company is more introvert, less outgoing. It will receive representatives of another firm but is unlikely to return the visit. There is, last of all, a difference in its attitude towards the young. In a female organization the maternal instinct is highly developed. Towards its offspring there is a protective attitude, a lenience which often goes beyond the bounds of its generally conservative finance.

In discussing the history of Merger, we find that the respectable alliance, arranged in advance and favoured by all the relatives, had its heyday between World Wars I and

II. Such was the current emphasis on the material aspects that sex was often apparently ignored. We must remember, in this connection, that the Slump of 1929–31 came in the middle of the period. After 1930, more especially, and until 1937 or later, the mergers were between firms which were suffering from depression. They fell into each other's arms, seeking consolation and help. There were other motives for Merger even then but the general picture is of tottering Companies clutching at each other for support during the blizzard. Whatever the circumstances of the union, many of the mergers which date from this period have been extremely successful. It is upon a study of this period that the *Parkinsey Report* is based. It is a monumental work, in two volumes, which it would be impossible even to summarize in such a chapter as this. To those volumes the reader may turn for a full account of corporate reproduction, with chapters on merger, on pre-mergital relationships, abnormalities and separation.

The second half of the Report has proved most generally acceptable. It deals with merger in a thorough and realistic manner, showing the value of a permanent partnership and tracing the steps by which it can be achieved. It is strongly emphasized that a perfect mutual Trust is impossible without a balanced disclosure on either side. If the one partner is liable to see red, it is futile for him to complain that the other's record is consistently black. The failings of either must be known, and it is wrong to imagine that a debit on one side can be set against a debit on the other. It is almost equally essential that both parties should be given a clean bill of health. A young firm which has been in a cartel at some time or other may turn out to be infected with long arrears.

Mention should be made of the section devoted to the birth of the subsidiary company—and Appendix Y, dealing with the problem of the illegitimate subsidiary, born outside merger. On the subject of subsidiary companies the author evidently believes that merger is incomplete without offspring. He does not go so far as to state that the absence of any subsidiary is proof in itself that the merger has failed. He adduces figures which prove, however, that the separation rate is appreciably higher among childless amalgamations and definitely lower when the subsidiaries number three or more. The proportion of mergers which end in disaster has risen steadily of recent years and we glimpse in this Report something of the wreckage to which many high hopes have been brought. Sometimes every effort is made to reconcile the parties. Every possible compromise is discussed. But the day comes when failure has to be frankly admitted. The merger ends in the divorce court and a fatherless subsidiary company is left to grow up as a juvenile deliquident.

The *Parkinsey Report* is in a class by itself and represents a great advance on all previous work. The strictly scientific approach presents the whole subject in a clear light, freed from prejudice and pruriency. It remains a question whether this work is fit for the open shelves; whether it should be available, for example, to very young firms at the outset of their business career. Opinions about this will inevitably differ but people of courage and vision will conclude, perhaps, that there is no virtue in ignorance and that candour is best. Firms too young to know will be unable, in fact, to comprehend; while those with the urge to inquire are old enough to be informed. Nor can they turn for information to any more comprehensive work than this.

Behind the whole Victorian effort to protect the young lady and especially the heiress, lay the fear of elopement. The romantic character of this practice is well established in fiction. We all know the procedure—the bribed maid-servant, the love letter, the girl at the window, the young man in the moonlight, the assignation in the churchyard, the ladder, the flight, the pursuit, the marriage. What the Victorians feared, however, was not so much the runaway match as the sordid betrayal. Sequel to the real elopement was the demand for money. For a substantial sum the blackmailer would return the girl unharmed and un-married. For an even larger sum the blackmailer would agree to marry the girl he had already seduced. In either event the victim's family was involved in anxiety, discredit and expense; thus providing an example which other families would be all the more eager to avoid. Similar to this bugbear of an earlier generation, less familiar today, is the Takeover Bid of the twentieth century. Among Limited Liability Companies the Takeover Bid is the equivalent of the Elopement or Seduction. In more con-servative business circles it is looked upon with a mixture of fascination and horror, disapproval and envy. However, the Takeover Bid does not lead of necessity to an unhappy merger. The fact must be faced, though, that the Bidder is usually polygamous. He has a harem, with wives, concu-bines, children and grandchildren. This is called a Group and is remarkable these days for the variety of its interests.

What are the commercial equivalents of the assignation, the ladder and the race for Gretna Green? These are best illustrated in dramatic form; a form in which weeks of negotiation can be conveniently compressed into minutes. The scene, let us suppose, is the Boardroom of Doolittle &

Hording, the Company which controls a chain of 250 grocery stores. The portraits of Doolittle and Hording look down with approval on their sons-in-law, Dooless and Hordmore, the Company's Chairman, respectively, and Treasurer. The other Directors present are Hidewell, Fusty and Lacking. The room is decorated in lilac and silver with chilly daffodils on light oak and a slightly feminine taste in curtains. The company is long established, female, conservative and undervalued. In one corner is a bronze statue of Constipation by Rodin. As the curtain rises we find the Directors in a state of twittering panic, with the Chairman on the 'phone.

CHAIRMAN: (*Into receiver*) Yes, I see . . . Quite . . . I realize that . . . But you feel reasonably sure? . . . Thanks, Dick. Good-bye. (*To the others*) Yes, our guess was correct. *Mayfair Investments* were buying our shares for Isaac Cottonwolf and the Mail Order Group. They probably hold 12 per cent of our equity.

HORDMORE: With the 20 per cent we hold, this Board can defy him.

LACKING: But he is still buying. The shares had risen again by eleven this morning.

HIDEWELL: Why should he pick on *us*?

FUSTY: What harm have we ever done?

CHAIRMAN: He wants our cash and our freeholds at a bargain price. And our shareholders (if they fall for it) will receive voteless 'A' shares in Mail Order. Oh, dear, what will become of us? (*Enter typist with note for the*

Chairman.) And now Cottonwolf is believed to own 16 per cent! There is nothing else for it. We shall have to raise the dividend.

DIRECTORS: (*Incredulous*) *Raise the dividend??*

HORDMORE: Unthinkable!

LACKING: But I don't see *why?*

CHAIRMAN: You don't see anything. We must declare an interim dividend of 8 per cent.

HORDMORE: But that would make 15 *per cent* for the year! What about our reserves? What about our depreciation account?

CHAIRMAN: It is a hard decision but we have no alternative. Agreed?

ALL: (*Reluctantly*) Suppose so. . . .

CHAIRMAN: (*Telephoning*) Tell the shareholders that we are paying an interim dividend of 8 per cent. Add that our prospects are terrific! (*To the others*) That should do the trick! (*Telephone rings.*) Yes, Dooless here. What? *What's* that? . . . Oh, thanks. (*To the others*) The shareholders don't believe that we shall pay as good a dividend after Cottonwolf has withdrawn. He now holds 19 per cent of the equity!

HORDMORE: But of *course* we shan't pay 15 per cent after the crisis is over! I hope that is understood?

CHAIRMAN: It is understood by the shareholders all right. . . . (*Telephone rings.*) Good heavens! . . . Yes, Mr Cottonwolf. . . . You are making a formal offer? . . . How

much? ... Fifty-two shillings? ... Do I accept? Nonsense.
I must put your proposal to the Board ... (*To the others*)
Do we accept? (*They all shake their heads.*) No, we do *not*
accept. We defy you! What is more, sir, we feel sure that
the shareholders will take our advice and refuse to sell!
(*Rings off. Makes a call.*) Tell the shareholders that the
Board advises them not to sell. (*Rings off.*)

HORDMORE: Remember, Dooless, that we hold 20 per
cent of the shares between us. He cannot gain the 90 per
cent he needs to make the rest sell, and his offer is conditional on that; or so I assume.

CHAIRMAN: It *is* conditional, as you say. And many of
the shareholders will support us.

FUSTY: But how many?

CHAIRMAN: (*Into receiver*) How many of the shareholders have agreed to accept Mr Cottonwolf's offer? ... I
see ... How many have rejected it? ... I see. Thank you.
(*To the others*) He now controls 43 per cent of the shares,
and we only 31 per cent. All we can do is offer a still higher
dividend. Shall we do that?

ALL: (*Gloomily*) Might as well.

CHAIRMAN: (*Into receiver*) Tell the shareholders that we
are raising the interim dividend to 12 per cent ... What's
that? No? Good God! (*To the others*) He has 47 per cent of
the shares. Let's see what effect our dividend has.

HIDEWELL: I don't see that it will have any.

FUSTY: I think it may backfire.

LACKING: But why? The shareholders ought to be

impressed. (*Clerk enters with evening paper which he lays before the Chairman.*) What's this?

CHAIRMAN: Good heavens! Cottonwolf says that shareholders will still receive the increased dividend even after he gains control. That is bound to influence them! Oh, dear! (*Into receiver*) How many shares do we control now? Is that all? And Cottonwolf? No! Really? Well, thanks for telling me. (*To the rest*) He holds 51 per cent and he has made his offer unconditional!

HORDMORE: (*Groaning*) He controls the Company!

FUSTY: (*Wailing*) He can replace the Board!

HIDEWELL: (*Sighing*) He can sell our freeholds and take the shops on a lease!

LACKING: Ah, but we can write to *The Times*! Yes, and we can ask for a Board of Trade Investigation!

CHAIRMAN: Don't deceive yourself, Lacking. We have been defeated. We must surrender and make the best terms we can.

Let this example be a warning. Takeovers will happen when least expected and no rising executive can afford to lose sight of the fact. When a merger takes place the advantage lies normally with the male Corporation, which has been acquisitive and active. It is to such a Corporation that the rising executive should attach himself, remembering that the reorganization which accompanies the merger will create opportunities for those who look ahead. Executives on the female side are more likely to be displaced and thrust aside. For them the future is indeed pregnant with trouble and they have only themselves to blame. Through ignorance of the facts they have found themselves on the wrong side of the merger. Theirs is a fate which others should seek to avoid. Always be on the male or active side. And when you come to hold high office, maintain at all costs the masculine character of your firm. Merge but never submerge.

THE THIRD LAW

Let us assume in this last chapter that you, the reader of this page, have gained one of the higher positions in the modern world. With the help of this book (thumbed and dog-eared beneath the pillow) you have gone from strength to strength. But pause for a minute. Where is it all taking you? What is the final goal?

Of course there are as many goals as there are people, but take as one example the Stupendic Gigantsome Metal Company, which has a capital of one billion billion and an industrial empire deployed from Iceland to Tasmania. The Stupendic came into existence (you will recall) as the result of a merger. The old Gigantsome Company (an amalgamation of Sabre Tooth, Tiger Ltd with Fluttering and Swoon Brothers) was taken over by Stupendic, Mammoth and Topless Ltd (itself the sequel to the purchase of Soaring, Cloudcapped and Dizzy by Bandersnatch, Clawtalon and Clutch). So the Stupendic Gigantsome has come to bestride the bleak landscape of the modern world. Millions stand within its shadow, looking to it for protection and livelihood. Whether as executives, technicians, shareholders or workers; whether as subsidiary allies, subcontractors, retailers or dependants, they all gaze upwards in mute adoration. Nor has their loyalty been thrown away, for Stupendic has provided many of them with all they dared to ask. This is today's Leviathan, the image before which its devotees are prostrate, the deity to which daily sacrifices are made, the throne before which petitions are cast.

But there are signs of revolt. Were you to wander un-noticed through London clubs and lobbies you would overhear the murmurings of sedition. There are people, you would gather, who think that Stupendic is too power-ful for the public good. The criticism you would hear on all sides is that the Stupendic does not do enough for the public welfare. It exists to make a profit for its share-holders and even more for its directors. It takes too much and contributes too little. It is a soulless machine doing nothing for the nation as a whole. Yet the Stupendic has the advantage—whatever its other faults—of being super-national. It is among the forces which work blindly for improved relationships between one country and another. This is a matter not of deliberate policy but of habitual outlook; the outlook of men whose business is worldwide. The model for supernational affairs is not to be found so much at Geneva or the Hague as in the boardroom of an Oil Company. The larger companies are not among the groups which clamour against war; and this is extremely fortunate, for conflict widens (as we all realize) in direct proportion to the demand for peace. But they do represent the international outlook as found among scientists, bankers and circus clowns. They are thus in several respects a power for good, having long since solved the sort of problem which the world's foreign ministers are still struggling to define.

The feeling must linger, however, that a disease is there. Among the employees you will note a trace of anxiety, an eagerness to justify themselves, an urge to liberalize the Company's policy. The period of ruthless competition has passed. The battle for supremacy is over. With prosperity assured, the time has come for high-minded patronage and public spirit. It is the company's aim to serve the people, or better still to serve mankind. One aspect of this growing liberality is represented by the professionalism of management. The manager of today adds to his professional training an atmosphere of professional etiquette. 'Is this good business?' may be his first question, and 'What is the tax angle?' his second, but 'Is it ethical?' is now the third. In times past the loftiest references to 'service' were the invariable preliminary to someone being swindled. This is no longer true. The ethics are often as ethical, or very nearly as ethical, as they sound. The business man takes his place alongside the judge, the preacher and the surgeon, being prevented by his cloth from doing this or that. To buy at the lowest price and sell at the highest is no longer the object in view. He asks only to serve the public to the best of his ability, showing a helpful benevolence towards his trade rivals (now few and unimportant), a generous paternalism towards the prime producers, a candid integrity towards the buying public. He is among the latest aspirants to professional status, full of management jargon to prove his special knowledge, full of Rotary Club idealism to prove his essential worth. The directors of Stupendic are among the most ethical of these very ethical men. The Stupendic contribution to many a cause has left the charitable organization prostrate, its officials unemployed and aimless. There is a scale of generosity that can practically kill.

Yet even if the Stupendic has a liberal outlook; is a good influence, far-sighted and generous; is internally minded and is guilty of none of the crimes of which it is accused; *it is still too big*. The process of integration, rationalization and absorption which brought the Stupendic into existence may seem inevitable in retrospect (and probably was), but the result is something too ponderous to survive. Like the vanished dinosaurs the Stupendic has become too cumbersome to adjust itself to change.

The complexity of the Stupendic Gigantsome is apparent from its organization chart, its hierarchy, its rigidity, its uniformity. And what people fail to realize is that the complexities derive not from policy but merely from size. Given the mere numbers and distances involved, the complex organization becomes inevitable. Decisions become impersonal and distant, attributable not to a person but to 'Them'. It may be the Board's action but on whose advice? With complexity comes the need for rules and precedents. With it comes the tide of paperwork, the statistics and returns. With it, finally, comes the effort to be alike. There are people, it is true, who have taken fright about the organization man. There are industrial leaders who would like to reverse the trend. But this uniformity comes not from fashion but from the nature of things. If personnel are to be interchangeable, they *must* be alike. They must be prefabricated to a standard pattern. How else can the system work? The pattern is complicated enough as it is. To introduce the variables associated with personality would make it impossible. In light fiction it is assumed that a retired British Colonel must conform to an accepted pattern (Dammit! What?) just as Generals must be choleric and professors absent-minded. Part of the old army officer's usefulness lay in the fact that commanders could be replaced without any perceptible change in outlook, discipline or routine. So it is with the executive sent to Honolulu by the Intercontinental Oil Company. Arriving as successor in oilsmanship to someone whose training is identical, he carries on smoothly from the point where his predecessor left off. The replacement of one peppery and whiskered Colonel by another, the succession of one 'oilminded' executive by the next, these are the sort of changes observable in the Palace forecourt where the sentries may be relieved but the colourful ritual remains the same.

Most of the Giant Company's complexity is the result of size. But some of its complexity is the result of age. Few of the big Companies are still under their founder's presidency. By this stage one of two things has happened. Either a grandson of the founder is Chairman, with a dynastic title like Rothsfeller III or else the management has passed into the hands of the experts. In either event the initial momentum will have been lost. Rothsfeller III lacks, as a rule, the ruthless virility of Rothsfeller I. He lacks the original propellent—the urge to escape from poverty or social disadvantage. He offers, instead, the picture of authority, dignity, culture and charm. For governing an established empire—one he could never have acquired—the Third in line can be very well fitted indeed. But what about the fourth? As in all monarchies, the moment comes when the successor to the throne is a weakling, an intellectual, a sportsman or aesthete. Control passes inevitably to the experts, the efficiency men, the figureheads of the managerial revolution.

A figurehead, in this modern sense, is a head full of figures. The present Managing Director of Stupendic rose to that high office by application, knowledge, loyalty, foresight, hardness, persistence and luck. The one quality he never had or wanted was the quality of leadership. Some of his rivals had it and were long since discarded as insubordinate. For running the organization he had all that he needed: ability, health, versatility and strength.

But now his labours have been brought to an end. And however he goes, whether through illness, accident or age, you will be chosen to succeed him; provided you have so far followed the author's advice. How does it come about? Very simply. The most influential member of the Board will use 'the old boy net', telephoning a leading figure in the financial world. After each name (other than yours) there will be just that pause on the end of the wire that will tell him all that he needs to know. Your name need never be mentioned. But the thing is done and the post is yours. After a lifetime of effort, you have arrived. And beneath the shining efficiency of your deep-carpeted office you will sense, if alert, the signs of woodworm and dry rot, fungus and rust. You will hear the death-watch beetle's stealthy approach. Are there too many, you wonder, on the Board of Directors? Are the initials too numerous on each invoice and bill? Is everyone too specialized and secretive? Is there too wide a distribution of documents and memoranda? Is the prevailing complacency enough to suffocate? Is the hearse actually at the door?

What confronts you is not disorganization but decay. Decadence is something, therefore, which you need to understand. You may associate decadence in your mind with black satin pyjamas and absinthe, remarking (and correctly) that Stupendic is comparatively free from both. But that is to misunderstand the nature of decay. When a tree decays it is not normally from sickness and never (one assumes) from sin. It decays because it has reached

its maximum growth, maintaining that size and weight for the period usual with that type of tree. It cannot live for ever in any case, and institutions, whether political or industrial, are not essentially different. For them too, maturity leads to decay.

So it is with Stupendic Gigantsome. Its growth is finished. It could, in theory, absorb its chief rival in a final merger. This, however, may be prevented by law. Nor would it always seem advisable even as a matter of policy. The better plan is often to preserve the appearance of competition while discreetly agreeing on prices, wages and quality. So the Stupendic will retain its present share of the trade, expanding one branch and curtailing another, introducing automation where practicable and changing the angle of its advertising policy from time to time. It would seem to be one of the more permanent features of the industrial landscape. Its decay, neverthe-

184

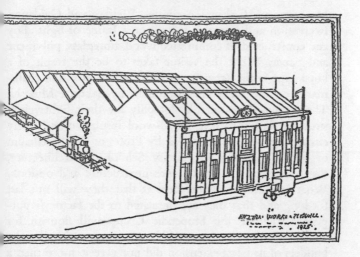

less, has begun, its progress showing more dignity than vigour.

Why is this? Stupendic has fallen a victim to Parkinson's Third Law: *Expansion means complexity, and complexity decay*. Signs of decay are everywhere. Look afresh at the buildings. First, there is the original shed of 1912 in which the enterprise began, now a museum. Next there is the factory building of 1925, vast, sprawling, and impatiently thrown together; a mere roof over the machines. Then you have the Head Office of 1934, built after the great merger and replete with marble and bronze, wrought iron and oak. Across the highway are the frantic extensions of 1944, fulfilling the purpose of all temporary buildings, which is to occupy for fifty years a site that is wanted for something else. Finally, there is the latest structure, built in 1960 to house the new departments; Public Relations, Personnel

185

Management, Cultural Activities, Welfare and Guidance, Recreation and Sport. It is built on a frame of light alloy and constructed of compressed wood, fibreglass, polythene and paper. What the visitor takes to be the result of a burst pipe is the Japanese Garden. What look like chalk-marks on the walls are the murals by Sakuma Musashi. The premises are notable not only for their lightweight structure but for their wood-wool insulation and freely circulating hot air. Designed by Professor Schnitzelbaum of the Wotchester University School of Architecture, they represent the latest trends in structure and outlook. What is manifest about them is that they will not last for long and that they are unrelated to the factory's purpose. Whether the Stupendic Group will flourish for another twenty years may still be an open question but the builders of its latest extension did not give it more than a decade.

Having looked at the buildings, send for the salaries list and see what value the Corporation sets on enterprise. Executives are broadly of two kinds, those technically capable of starting something new and those merely able to administer the organization that exists. Which is the more important—a new product or a smooth procedure? There is usually some lip-service to innovation and progress but the real scale of values is expressed in the salary cheques. Who matters more, the engineer or the accountant, the chemist or the clerk? Did the Works Manager gain office by discovering the possibilities of a by-product or by running a department without friction? Both types of ability may be valued but which is valued more? Where the highest value is placed on routine competence, the process of decay has begun.

Last of these preliminaries, visit the most remote outpost of the Stupendic Empire, the experimental farm in Iceland or the research unit in Tasmania. Discover what the scientists are doing and then ask them the crucial question: when were you last visited by a director of the firm? If the answer is 'Last year' the situation is bad. If the answer is 'In 1958' the situation is worse. If the answer is 'Never' the situation is almost beyond remedy. For while decay at the centre may take the form of fussy interference, this is consistent with a neglect of things more distant. The running down of the central machine will be manifest first in the peripheral areas, the places to which central authority can barely extend. It is at the farthest of these —on the Hadrian's Wall, as it were, of a declining Empire —that the breakdown is most obvious. That the cohorts there are under strength is less significant than the fact that no one has come to inspect them. The Empire may still exist but its energy is dwindling and will presently vanish. Where this is happening the process of decay is well advanced.

What is the remedy to be? The answer is contained in the one word 'Leadership'. And what is leadership, what is this secret which each generation must discover afresh?

It is the art of so indicating a distant goal as to make all else seem trivial. When the natural leader has finished describing the Holy Grail, the Eternal City, the Glory of France or the Honour of the Regiment, all immediate privations and perils are thought irrelevant. It was with something of the same fervour that old Ben Bandersnatch called his men about him on the eve of the first great merger. 'Boys,' he said, 'we must think big. If this deal goes through, we shall control a quarter of the industry!'

Who, in the light of his enthusiasm, could have asked for a salary raise? Who on the assembly floor could have begun discussing a thirty-hour week? Who complained, for that matter, if kept at the office all night? It was reward sufficient to come home, white and haggard, vowing your wife to secrecy. 'Don't tell anyone, Susan, but Old Ben is on the warpath. I think he's brought it off. The news should be all over the world on Thursday. Gosh, I'm worn out!' Assume, if you like, that Susan's husband had nothing to do with the deal. Suspect, if you will, that he was not even wanted at the office. The fact remains that he was living in the presence of a drama beside which his own affairs could be forgotten. This was the mood in which men fought at Austerlitz, Trafalgar or the Normandy Beachhead. It is under an inspired leader that the soldier comes to regard his own possible death as a mere incident. It is under an industrial leader that the workman can grudge his own wage as a debit figure in the firm's tottering finances. At least in the early and adventurous phase of an industry, the excitement can mean more to people than the pay. 'In those days,' they can boast afterwards, 'Men were *Men*.' But those days of adventure are long ago. The mere size of the organization has created complexity, and with complexity has come the rule of gravity; so weightily expressed in ponderous speech, in set ways, in certain mental attitudes, above all in argument. And gravity has won.

The situation is one which might be compared, superficially, with that faced by a hotel proprietor who has returned, after a long absence, to find the hotel neglected. The rooms are dirty and the paintwork has suffered, the service is bad and the food is worse. Servants who are perfectly capable of good work have picked up idle and slovenly habits. There are several possible remedies but the quickest and most effective is to announce a cocktail party for two hundred guests, to be followed (after three days) by a Banquet and (two days later) by a Ball. Cooks, waiters and barmen suddenly find themselves faced by a major crisis, with problems as numerous as they seem insoluble. Their morale rises overnight and the hotel becomes a different place. Any other organization can be at least temporarily revived in the same way.

Can you re-create, by such means, the sense of adventure and hazard? Can you rally Stupendic to face the eventual competition of people elsewhere who work instead of argue, of people to whom progress means more than just a longer weekend? This you can do, provided only that you have remained, by some miracle, young at heart. For success goes to the young and youth is the knowledge that there are new worlds to conquer and that there is always time for change. No matter how old you are, youth is a possession you can keep if you choose. It can be there for all to see—in the spring of your step, in your quick readjustment to changed circumstances, in your willingness to take a risk, in your readiness to laugh. Those who know what decay is and are prepared for its onset can be free, for their lifetime, from Parkinson's Third Law. Over them gravity has no hold. Not for them—and not for you —that solemn adherence to the Company's pattern, that burden of complaint, that weary dignity of age. You can take things lightly if you will, obeying rather the rule of levity: the rule that has landed you, and will keep you, at the top.

But . . . no organization can last for ever. Even while

you are displaying all your gifts of leadership and saving Stupendic in the nick of time, another and a younger man has his foot in the door of another and more virile organization. His present desk is his first. He almost seems to live at the office. His career has just begun.